1

Waking The Lion Within

Waking The Lion Within

Reclaiming Your Position In Christ

Nelson L. Schuman

Dedication

To everyone in the world that grew up either without a father or with a father who did not model strong spiritual character and lacked full confidence and strength of walking in his complete and loving authority of Jesus Christ causing his children to be weak in the Lord and unsure how to lead their own families in Christ.

Endorsements

"I love Nelson's rich boldness in how he leads other men and women to achieve their own confidence and bold faith in their own lives. He is truly a spiritually strong man of God that is changing the lives of thousands to become who they are in Christ. His heart for helping people change from weak individuals to powerful leaders is amazing. I am thankful to the Lord for connecting me to Nelson."

Tim Brown – Sr. Pastor, New Life Assembly of God,

Noblesville, IN

"This book challenges men to stand up for their convictions and to lead as Christ has instructed them to. It is another wake-up call to the men of this generation to follow the Holy Spirit."

Owen Mason – Lead Pastor, Church Alive,

Lafayette, IN

"Have you gone along with things just to avoid confrontation? Is someone in your life calling all the shots, exploiting your position in life, but you say 'ok' rather than deal with the backlash? It's time to reclaim your position of authority in Christ? Find your boldness and live the life that God intended for you. Nelson has shown us the truth!"

David Natali – Sr. Pastor, Turning Point Ministries,

Carmel, IN

Testimonies

"Waking the Lion Within is truly a book that every man needs to desperately read and live out every day. It is time to replace the tepidness and lack of boldness with that of a lion who roars with no fear and total confidence in Christ causing the enemy to run from them."

"I grew up with a father that was weak spiritually and modeled a powerless life in the Lord. He went through the motions of taking his family to church, but rarely cracked open his Bible and never taught me how to truly be a man of God. After reading Waking the Lion Within, I finally have seen a breakthrough in my life and will NEVER go back to the old weak Ahab that I was."

"I have been married for fifteen years and have three children. I am sorry to admit that I let my wife try to lead our family spiritually and unfortunately, it has led to a real mess in our family. I abdicated my Godly responsibility to lead spiritually and now have a price to pay for allowing my children to be lukewarm for the Lord. Thank you so much for writing this powerful book to help me wake up to become like Christ and see miracles and power that I never knew was possible."

"I am a woman and am forty-five years old. I grew up with a father that lacked the spiritual leadership that our family needed. I have struggled with walking in the power and authority of Christ and after reading your book, I have learned that even though my husband is to be the true head spiritually, I also needed a kick in my pants to be a powerful mighty woman of God. You are so right that praying in tongues helps us to energize our spirits into who we really are in Christ. Thank you so much for writing this much needed book at this time."

"It is time to change the men in this world from weak Ahab's who serve their flesh into powerful men of God who press into the things of the spirit, and live lives pure and righteous before the Lord. We should all be walking in seeing people healed and delivered through us and giving prophetic words. Thank you for challenging me to ratchet up my life to a whole new level."

"As a pastor, I have seen so many men that want to change and become powerful in the Lord but just do not know how to do it since their own fathers never modeled it for them. Thanks for helping me in my job of getting men to transform from Ahab's to Elijah's and Elisha's."

Acknowledgements

I want to thank all those in my life that have helped encourage me to press in and onward and upward in Christ. Without my closest friends supporting me and being there when I needed someone, I do not know what I would have done to get to the other side of my destiny in the Lord. I love you all!

I also want to thank Chris Schuman for his meticulous editing of my book that will ultimately change the lives of people from a spiritual weakling to one of bold confidence knowing who they are in Christ. You are an extremely detailed and diligent man with an eye for perfection and I am honored to call you my brother.

I want to especially thank all of my family and friends that the Lord has brought into my life who truly love me unconditionally and know my heart and compassion to help people with all I am capable of through Christ to live a life aligned with the power and love of the Lord. You are all awesome and I love you for your support and dedication:

(Aggie, Alan, April, Ashley, Austin, Becca, Bill, Bob, Brandon, Brian, C, Carrie, Cassia, Cindy, Charles, Chris, Chuck, Courtney, David, Dawn, Deborah, Duane, Elaine, Erin, Garry, George, Gina, Hannah, Keith, James, Jan, Jana, Jess, Jessica, Joe, John, Jordan, Judy, Julie, Larry, Luke, Marshall, Marvin, Megan, Michael, Michelle, Misty, Neil, Nick, Nova, Owen, Patti, Patty, Paul, Phil, Priscilla, Randy, Remon, Robia, Ron, Sharell, Steve, Sue, Taylor, Tiffany, Todd, Tyler, and Tim)

Table of Contents

INTRODUCTION

We are all called to be like Christ – to love unconditionally, be at peace with people, help those who are hurting, walk boldly without fear in who we are in Christ and if you are a man, you are called to be the spiritual head of your wife and family while if you are a woman, you are called to respect and support your husband while also walking in full confidence of who you are in Christ. If that is the case, why are there so many Christian men who are not leading spiritually in their families and relinquishing their God required duties to their wives while serving their fleshly desires of watching sports excessively, going to bars, putting their vocations and work first, and not pressing into the things spiritually that can change their families and children to become strong and mighty men and women of valor? There is definitely something wrong in the church today and the enemy is behind all of this dysfunction, confusion, lack of leadership, disappointment, and frustration.

Over the years, I have met some really good men who are very honest, loving, and helpful yet they are unable to live their lives the way the Lord would have them when it comes to leading their families spiritually. I have also seen many men who have high levels of strife in their lives with wives who sometimes behave exceedingly controlling over them. I have also met some very loving and submissive wives who are unable to enjoy a peaceful marriage with their husbands due to their husbands being excessively controlling. Their husbands may lord over them twisted Bible verses in order to get their selfish way and instead of loving them like Christ loved the church, they control them in a manner completely contrary to the way a man of God should love. The common denominator in all these marriages is that the meek and mild men and women grew up with fathers who were weak spiritual leaders or non-existent altogether and relinquished all their responsibility to the Lord in order to live more for their flesh and worldly desires. Many of their fathers may have been considered "good men" or "good 'ol boys" by those in the church, but they were not strong spiritual leaders in their families due to myriad reasons of which normally was because their own fathers abdicated their responsibility of leading their families spiritually before them. Once the cycle starts, it becomes extremely challenging to break as one fathers son or daughter begets another son or daughter who struggles with being strong in the Lord and leading spiritually.

Men are supposed to be the spiritual head of their wives and families when it comes to the Lord, but from my experience - I only see about 10-15% of men that actually do this in the way the Lord expects and lays out in the Word. The majority of men abdicate this extremely important responsibility and either the wife takes over or no one does and the family flounders and thus we are experiencing the mess that we see in society all over the world today. I have talked to many men who know that they should lead spiritually and desperately want to but just cannot do it, and they do not understand why. I have learned exactly why and will explain in this book how to break free from your past and to awaken the lion within you that wants to be bold and roar with the same authority that Jesus Christ calls us to.

I am not talking about behaving in any way abusively or overly controlling but am talking about the proper way a man is to lead his family (or a woman is to be assertive in a supportive way to her husband while kicking the enemy's butt everywhere she goes). No person should be a doormat and have their spouse control and walk all over them because we are all called to be bold in Christ and our faith, and there is a powerful freedom when we know that we know who we are in Christ and are not afraid of the enemy anymore. The challenge is when our earthly father does not model a strong faith for us which affects so many generations of people thereafter for years and years to come. I recently had a man approach me after I spoke about my testimony at his church one Sunday morning. He said that the biggest thing that stuck with him during the seventy minutes that I shared was that he needed to learn how to lead and grow in his spiritual walk and to walk in the same boldness as Christ. He did not know how to walk in his authority in Christ because his father never modeled it for him. He wanted to become more like what I was discussing and how I had changed from a weak man into more of a lion within - but needed to learn how. Everything in his spirit was crying out to become the mighty man of valor that the Bible talks about, yet it was extremely hard for him because he never saw his own father live his life that way.

From my experience, I would estimate that 80-85% of the men in church never had good models of a strong godly man in their lives and that is why we have seen the denigration of society (in general), all over the world. It is understandable why a non-believer would see issues in their spiritual leadership abilities in their lives but for those who attend church on a regular basis, to struggle continually is very disappointing and sad. Most of the men in church today had fathers who also attended church, but they were never interested in the things of the spirit to a strong degree and if their fathers could not lead, then how would you expect their children to be strong in the Lord?

I have also met many men who were married to extremely controlling women and in most cases, these men were very godly men - yet they all had fathers that were weak leaders spiritually and were very weak and controllable. Thus, they married women who were strong and controlling who were often similar to their own mothers who controlled their fathers. The saying that 'a man will marry his mother' is very true. Unfortunately, the reason why men marry unhealthy and/or controlling women is because they do not want to lead spiritually. In doing so, they abdicate what the Lord commands them to do giving that responsibility over to their wives in order to pursue fleshlier desires. Once the mold has been cast, it is very difficult for the man to change into the bold and mighty man of valor that the Lord calls him to be.

Thus, it is the purpose of this book to help men become stronger leaders spiritually to their wives and children, and ultimately speak into the lives of other men who are in their sphere of influence. There are some women that can be extremely weak and have challenges becoming the leader that they should become for their children. They may also struggle with teaching other women to become who they are to be in Christ and this book will help to break them free from that as well. All of us need to become strong in the Lord and tell the enemy where to go because if we don't - the enemy will ruin our lives, destroy our marriages, and hurt our children. It is time to become who we were really created to be, a lion who roars and strikes fear into the enemy while walking boldly every day with no fear in our lives. We are to love everyone like Christ loved the church and be pure and spotless before the Lord with no hidden sin in our lives. We are also called to heal the sick, cleanse the lepers, cast out demons, and raise the dead. How many have you prayed for that have actually been healed instantly after you prayed? How many people have you either cast demons out of, or led through prayers to command demons out of themselves? It is time to walk boldy and learn your authority in Christ so that you can do all the things that the Lord has called you to do. You can and must do it because if you do not, then you will be held accountable by the Lord and you do not want Him to not be able to say, "Well done, my good and faithful servant." It is time to become strong and courageous!

22

CHAPTER 1

Who's Your Daddy?

When thinking about how our lives get shaped into developing who we become and how we behave from a spiritual perspective, one cannot fail to think about the major importance of having our earthly father model it for us. Sadly, and for the majority of us - we did not have a great example showing us how to master this extremely important responsibility during our growing up years from the time we were young to maturing into adulthood. This explains why we see so many people struggling to know exactly what should be done in order to walk powerfully in who they are to be in Christ and thus, leaves an entire world largely spiritually void. Most of the generations had fathers who were busy working in their jobs and careers, and trying to advance themselves and make more money for their families. They focused on providing material things and make an easier life for themselves so they could retire from work and not have to worry about financial concerns later in life. Unfortunately, the enemy did a great job of getting our men's minds off of spiritual, life-giving desires and onto material concerns and allowed an entire generation to be void of most all things godly. Other fathers struggled to just make enough money to provide food for their families, much less thinking of how to walk in their authority in Christ due to their challenges with the lack of a proper role model in their life. Their walk with the Lord suffered due to the lack of time that they had available to draw near to Him, and their reliance on themselves became greater than trusting the Lord to provide for their needs. Unfortunately, by taking our eyes off of the Lord and putting them on our current circumstances, we lost all faith that the Lord would provide supernaturally for all our needs; so the enemy was able to use our fear for financial provision and our tendency to look in envy at our neighbor's cars and homes to pull us away from our real provider, Jehovah Jireh.

Many fathers back in the 1950's and 60's in the United States would often take their families to church and tried to lead what would be an acceptable "godly" appearing lifestyle, but few were really tuned in and received direction from the Lord on a regular basis. Therefore, when their children observed them every day dealing with life decisions, they never saw a man who was able to hear from God nor trusted completely in the Lord. They knew that they were supposed to behave acceptably, which usually meant not having sex before marriage and once married, to stay married and not divorce. If there were disagreements in marriage, you were to work things out and not even mention the D word. Unfortunately, the men would either go to church and not listen to the message because most if it was boring to them and they couldn't see how to apply it, or they would just stop going to church and stay home to watch golf, football, baseball, basketball, or do something else that their flesh was desiring.

When it came to understanding (at a deep level) why people did the things they did, very few to none talked about the prevalence of how demonic spirits affected them. The expansion of psychologists and psychiatrists became more prevalent as people tried to understand why people behaved in ways that were not normal. Trying to have discussions and counsel people to behave more "normally" developed into a profession of counseling and from well-meaning Christian people trying to help people, but they did not understand the invisible world of spirits and how they controlled humans by speaking to them and getting them to behave in ways that caused people pain. More and more doctors and psychologists and the whole mental health world dealt with people the only way they knew how and that was through medication which never got to the root of their issues and caused many more side effects including suicide. Today, we are at an all-time high with medicating people to try to deal with spiritual issues. Those who are forced to take stronger medication have to deal with all the side effects due to spirits of Pharmakeia affecting people. What a mess this world has become.

Unfortunately, due to fathers from the past not knowing their authority in Christ - we now are experiencing an epidemic of people who are behaving in ways that are out of control, desperate, depressed, over medicated, and are running around in fear instead of walking in the boldness and authority of Christ. Fathers abdicated their responsibility in learning what it was to lead their families spiritually and gave it to either their wives to take over or to no one. As a result, the state of the average family in the world today has a large percentage of homes that have no fathers or have fathers who do not know how to listen to the Lord and lead from a godly perspective. Also, the United States' women's movement of the late 1960's and 70's that developed into feminism began to usurp what God designed in that men no longer would lead so women decided they must take over many aspects in society and that they no longer needed a husband with many decreeing "I will submit to NO man!" The enemy pounced on this and the emasculation of men ensued causing them to feel like if they attempted to stand up for what was right, they were coming against women instead of the real enemy of the devil.

Thus, when men no longer pressed into the things from the Lord, the enemy increased the strategy of using women to be the new spiritual leaders which proliferated a spirit of control and manipulation over men that was not what the Lord designed from the start of the world. This resulted in men who would now be forced to submit to their wives and take their seats in servitude. What we are dealing with today are men who have lost their spiritual boldness and godliness in being able to lead their wives and families in the things of the Lord. Their backbone has been weakened and their voice is silent or barely whispering. They have been feminized into submission by the enemy into a position of spiritual weakness. They know in their hearts that this is not right, but they do not know how to "right the ship" - so to say, and change direction in their lives to get back on track. They cannot hear from the Lord, are unsure how vocal they should be in their beliefs so as not to upset their spouse or boss at work, feel hopeless that they could ever be looked at as a bold man of God like Moses or Elijah, and do not know many other men who they can talk to in order to be properly mentored.

I have met so many men who walk around aimlessly in their spiritual lives because they rarely open up in candid conversations with other men. Those who are in leadership, often times – are very soft spoken and gentle by nature (which is not a horrible trait to have, by the way) but are not confident in who they are in Christ and have never been taught on how to walk in the authority of Christ and what that means. Their wives "wear the pants in the family" and they don't know how to take the proper godly authority that the Lord has called them to have. Women do not really want to be the spiritual leaders of the home to their children, but if men are not going to take their rightful positions - they feel someone has to do it (can I get an "Amen" from the women who I know are reading this book!).

Therefore, the reason why a man is unable to walk in his Christ designed authority he was supposed to have from a spiritual perspective is due to his father not knowing how to do it. His father never did before him, and so forth and so on, and from generation to generation prior. When you have so many generations of men that do not know how to lead spiritually, how do you break free and start leading? Why is it so hard for a man to step up and become who Christ called them to be? This is not only a male issue since many women are also passive when it comes to walking in Christ boldly as they should. How can any person change to being more confident in whom they are in Christ when they have never seen it modeled for them?

That is what this book's goal is – to help you change from a life of spiritual passivity and weakness into a new life of walking every day with the ability to hear the Lord speak direction to you while also having no fear in every decision that you make and to not be held back by a lack of confidence of who you really are in Christ. The Lord does not want His people to have the enemy dictate to you what He wants you to be. The Lord has designed us to roar like a mighty lion, which is not afraid of anything while also being humble, pure, and loving at all times.

Most people think of the word meekness as being submissive or weak, but it actually means strength under control. That is what Jesus stood for, walked out, and modeled for us every day. When it came time for Him to give up His life, He showed the power that He possessed as the 300+ soldiers came to arrest him. John 18:3-6 NKJV states, "³ Then Judas, having received a detachment of troops, and officers from the chief priests and Pharisees, came there with lanterns, torches, and weapons. ⁴ Jesus therefore, knowing all things that would come upon Him, went forward and said to them, 'Whom are you seeking?' ⁵ They answered Him, 'Jesus of Nazareth.' Jesus said to them, 'I am He,' And Judas, who betrayed Him, also stood with them. ⁶ Now when He said to them, 'I am He,' they drew back and fell to the ground." Thus Jesus' words "I am He" caused over 300 soldiers to fall to the ground. He had all this power yet allowed Himself to be arrested without stopping it. He willingly gave up His life while having over twelve legions of angels at his disposal (over 72,000 angels and just one angel of the Lord killed 185,000 Syrians in one

night in 2 Kings 19:35). This is what the word 'meekness' means –
strength under control. We must always be in control of our emotions
and not lash out in anger no matter where we are (if someone cuts you
off in traffic or slows you down – do you speak disparaging words out
or do you stay calm and slow down without saying a word?). Yes,
Jesus did show more aggressive emotion and righteous indignation
when he cleared out the buyers and sellers in his Father's temple that
had been turned into a marketplace, but He did not strike anyone and
there is no time in His life that He ever hurt anyone physically. Jesus
was able to convey His wisdom in what needed to be shared while
controlling His behavior and walking in love and peace. He could
speak the truth in love. Sometimes people do not want to be told the
truth, but it is all in how we speak it that matters.

When we can actually walk in the same authority as Jesus
Christ and do the same things He did and greater (John 14:12 NKJV
"Most assuredly, I say to you, he who believes in Me, the works that
I do he will do also; and greater works than these he will do, because
I go to My Father."), then we should be doing exactly that. It will be
a process to go from walking in a lack of spiritual authority and
possibly being controlled by our spouse, to changing things in order
to break free from that control and growing in the Spirit of who you
really are in Christ. There is nothing in the world like the feeling of
commanding like Christ and seeing someone get healed instantly from
a broken bone, seeing a shorter leg grow out, having cancer dissolve
from inside their body, or giving a word of knowledge and/or
prophetic word that unlocks the future direction of a hurting person.
It will change your life forever. The first time you command a
demonic spirit to leave a boy who has been out of control for ten years
and then he changes instantly and becomes a nice, loving, and kind
child for his parents (who now have tears running down their cheeks
in eternal thankfulness to the Lord), is an experience that will be
seared into your memory and change you forever to serve Him. You
can and must become who you really are in Christ – the boldness of a
lion whose roar causes the enemy to run from you and your family.

CHAPTER 2

Lack of Faith

When a child grows up without a strong, loving, and godly father in their life, it profoundly impacts him or her for the rest of their life unless they have an encounter with the Lord to change what is in motion. Most children who grew up not seeing their fathers read their Bible consistently, model Christ-like behavior or hear them pray strong prayers in the same authority Christ teaches have struggles in their teenage and young adult years. It is very hard to be a powerful man or woman of God when your parents never showed you the way by their everyday life because you will simply become a product of your environment.

What happens to a child when they become a teenager and young adult coming from a typical family that just attended church and went through the motions without a real personal relationship with the Lord? Typically, you will see a son or daughter who develops into a nice young adult but does not hear from the Lord nor see any miracles or life changing experiences with the Lord, so they do not have a close, personal relationship that feels real. It is a bland, basic life of going to church, comparing stories with friends about challenges in their lives, hoping that you do not get sick, and praying very general prayers that have little to no effectiveness in manifesting results. I know this because it was my personal life and everyone's around me as well.

I grew up with the expectation that I needed to go to church and surround myself with Christians to encourage me and tried to do the right things. I was taught to minimize my sinning but I never heard from the Lord and was meandering through life with no clear direction other than a moral compass. It was frustrating for me because I felt deep inside of my spirit like there was more to being a Christian than just attending church and limiting my sin as much as possible. It felt like when I would read my Bible and try to be good, there was some kind of external force on me causing me to get bored and wanting me not to believe that there was ever anything more out there to experience spiritually. All of my friends that attended the church that I went to that were in their early 20's were all trying to make as much money as they could to provide a nice lifestyle for themselves. Unfortunately, none of them were truly on fire for God or for more matters of the Spirit. I attended a large church in Carmel, IN that was growing, but no one saw any miracles consistently from their prayers and no one seemed to hear clearly from God even though I took classes to help me hear from the Lord such as 'Experiencing God' by Henry Blackaby. It was like a nice group of people that meant well but had no clue about the deeper things in the spirit world and how those spirits affected people's lives everyday nor how to stand strong against the enemy and walk in the power of Christ that was available to them. If everyone did not believe that demonic spirits could affect Christians, then how could they battle against them and command them to be gone from their lives?

Many people attend small group Bible studies and other studies from other Christian authors (Beth Moore, John Eldredge, etc), but I could never get excited about hanging around 10-14 other people who continued to talk about how worried they were in their lives about the future, health related concerns, issues with their children, or who complained about their relatives, etc. In my spirit, I wanted to be around people who were victorious in their lives and walked in the same powerful authority as Jesus Christ and what Paul said we could and should be doing in the New Testament. Unfortunately, the faith that I saw exhibited was significantly lacking something and I did not want everyone else's limited faith that never moved mountains and barely moved peanuts. They talked about how we should be powerful in the Lord, yet no one really walked in that authority and ended up being just all words with no resilience and conviction behind them. They did good things to love on other people such as bringing food to those who just had a baby or were sick, but no one prayed the way Christ told them to pray and thus they saw minimal positive results and were not any better off than anyone else that was not a Christian.

Therefore, my perspective of someone who was strong in their faith was a person who attended church and maybe believed for something in their life that would happen in the future such as God providing them with a better job or perhaps working things out for their spouse who separated from them to come back and have a good marriage. It was foreign to understand that a person could have any more faith than the basics; and again - I had never been around anyone who believed more than the typical man that I was friends with. Many that were sick with diseases or dying from cancer were hoping that they would be healed, and I counted that as faith, but none truly knew their authority in Christ to be able to command the disease to leave their bodies. They were like 95% of other Christians in their faith who did not really have the faith that Christ talked about in the Bible, and if you do not know any better than how can you expect anything more? It was like we lived hoping and praying for the best but preparing for the worst. When we live in fear that an affliction or disease could come upon our bodies, we are unaware that this is how the enemy can actually put sickness on us that will kill us early.

At that time in my life, if someone would have told me that I did not really have faith - I would have taken an offense and reacted angrily towards them because I thought I had lots of faith. Looking back, I can honestly say that I was clueless when it came to faith and so was everyone else (who I was friends with) that thought they all had faith. The definition of ignorance is incomprehension of, unawareness of, unconsciousness of, unfamiliarity with, inexperience with, lack of knowledge about, informal cluelessness about, lack of knowledge, or lack of education. So yes, my friends and I were totally ignorant of what true bold faith in spiritual things of the Lord meant. We did not know what we did not know. We knew nothing about how the enemy was affecting us, our spouse, our children, work, lives, etc. Our spiritual eyes were not open to seeing things in the spirit as to how the enemy whispered to us in order to tempt us to sin, cause us to argue or strive with our spouses, make poor decisions spiritually, and manipulate us like a puppet on strings.

We were completely blind to the things of the spirit in our lives. We could only see things that were in the physical and look upon behaviors and not realize what was behind the behavior causing it. We had pains in our bodies so the only way we all knew to get healed was to go to our family doctor or specialist to try to get cured. If there was something that we could not get healed from by our doctor, we would then ask other people to help pray for healings hoping that if enough people cried out to God on our behalf - maybe we would get lucky and receive a miracle. Unfortunately, their prayers hardly ever worked because they were not praying with the authority of Christ that we're given because they were never taught by their pastors (because they never knew about it). We did not know that all we had to do was command our healing the way Christ said in the Bible and it would manifest according to our awareness of our authority; because no one taught us about walking in the full authority in Christ. We never developed the complete understanding in our

32

spirits of what it meant to walk powerfully in the Lord in all of His power and authority. We had all grown up with fathers who did not understand this so never taught us. We were blind for all intents and purposes; just wandering around life being dictated to by the enemy while hoping and "praying" that nothing bad would happen to us.

So what does faith mean to you? The definition in the Bible is in Hebrews 11:1-12 NKJV, "[1] Now faith is the substance of things hoped for, the evidence of things not seen. [2] For by it the elders obtained a good testimony. [3] By faith we understand that the worlds were framed by the word of God, so that the things which are seen were not made of things which are visible. [4] By faith Abel offered to God a more excellent sacrifice than Cain, through which he obtained witness that he was righteous, God testifying of his gifts; and through it he being dead still speaks. [5] By faith Enoch was taken away so that he did not see death and was not found, because God had taken him; for before he was taken he had this testimony, that he pleased God. [6] But without faith it is impossible to please Him, for he who comes to God must believe that He is, and that He is a rewarder of those who diligently seek Him. [7] By faith Noah, being divinely warned of things not yet seen, moved with godly fear, prepared an ark for the saving of his household, by which he condemned the world and became heir of the righteousness which is according to faith. [8] By faith Abraham obeyed when he was called to go out to the place which he would receive as an inheritance. And he went out, not knowing where he was going. [9] By faith he dwelt in the land of promise as in a foreign country, dwelling in tents with Isaac and Jacob, the heirs with him of the same promise; [10] for he waited for the city which has foundations, whose builder and maker is God. [11] By faith Sarah herself also received strength to conceive seed, and she bore a child when she was past the age, because she judged Him faithful who had promised. [12] Therefore from one man, and him as good as dead, were born as many as the stars of the sky in multitude – innumerable as the sand which is by the seashore."

So this is the faith that God is talking about us possessing. Not looking upon circumstances such as – your son or daughter was diagnosed by your family doctor as having ADHD (or whatever disease dujour that is the latest) and then getting into fear and doubt and listening to everything the doctor says to do to try to get cured; hoping for the best and praying that God will "please" heal them. Rather, learning what your authority in Christ is and then commanding the infirmity to be gone just like Jesus did. Having faith to move mountains out of your way so that you can walk in power and authority all of your days on earth is such an amazing feeling of boldness and confidence. We are called to be more than a conqueror and not to cower in fear and worry to the enemy, or in our families.

When a person comes into alignment with the Lord at a stronger spiritual level and learns how to speak to their mountains from a position of heaven with power and authority instead of a position of fear (and pleading with God to do something), there is a powerful difference. There is a transformation that must take place in your mind which your spirit desperately wants to move you into, but the enemy is going to try to come against you from moving into this stronger level of faith. You have to break free from a lifetime of the old dead ways of doing things and come into the new way of the Holy Spirit's power. There is life and death in the power of your tongue and God wants you to speak life. Think about how this earth was formed. God spoke things into existence. Think about how Jesus healed people – He usually spoke to them and said "be healed" because He knew He carried authority and whatever He said had to manifest. We, as Christians - have access to that same power and authority but only if we know it, utilize it, and expect it.

In my own life, the Lord called me out of a church I was attending because most all the people did not have the level of faith that He was taking me into. I needed that level of faith in order to transform into and accomplish the ministry He had for me. Had I stayed around those people, they would have kept me down to what their limited faith level was instead of where the Lord needed me to be and have faith to help people who were affected by demonic spirits. It usually will take you taking a step of faith on your part to move onward and upward. In my case, the Lord took me completely out of the church for what turned out to be two full years. I was shocked because I went to church every month of my life and could not understand why I had to leave the church for an extended period of time. I had to trust that the Lord knew what He was doing (which he usually does).

Looking back, it was absolutely necessary in order for me to accomplish what the Lord ultimately needed me to do. I watched some good faith preachers on television and the internet that helped me grow in my spiritual walk and was mentored by a powerful man of God and his ministry team that heard clearly from the Lord at an extremely high level. I spent time hearing the Lord direct me and I had to endure some extreme, major spiritual warfare coming against me trying to stop me in all aspects of my relationships with my children and my wife.

I would not be deterred though and already knew the importance of not giving up and pressing in every day to overcome some extreme circumstances until I was ready to go back into a church. This time, I was prepared to help people learn from what I'd discovered and teach them to change their old faithless mindsets including helping many pastors wake up and learn about taking their authority in Christ. It felt very strange because I was no longer the person I was before. Everyone I met was in so much worry and fear and it was difficult being around them because they did not know about walking in the authority of Christ and I was no longer like them. I had transformed to becoming more like Christ in every way – loving people, seeing miracles, hearing the Lord, and speaking prophetically. I was so excited and wanted to help others be transformed to do the same thing in their lives.

Be aware that in order to become who the Lord has called you to be in Him, it may involve not only changing churches but changing friends. The enemy will use your old faithless relationships to keep you held back from the things the Lord wants to take you into. This is a challenge because many that are walking in minimal faith may speak words against you that cause you to feel mocked or made to feel like you are crazy. The enemy will do whatever he can to persuade you not to learn how to become powerful in Jesus and if he knows you are not strong in the Lord, he will attack you to try to get you to give up and go back to the familiar. Expect to have spiritual warfare come against you, but do not be persuaded because the spirit in you knows what the right thing is to do. It is time to put on your helmet of salvation, breastplate of righteousness, and sword of the Spirit on and go into battle and take no prisoners. To become the spiritual effective leader you need to be will require you to take off the old man and put on the new.

CHAPTER 3

Marrying Your Mom

It is amazing to see how true it is, when speaking with men all around the world - how so many decide to marry women who are very similar to their own mothers. I have seen the following scenario played out many times over and over everywhere: Four brothers have grown up in the same family and have a father that is spiritually weak and mild but partnered with a wife who is strong, controlling, manipulative, and takes the lead spiritually. As the brothers grow up, they start to date girls who are similarly strong, controlling, and some may be leaders spiritually. The women enjoy the relationship with the sons because they know they can control the timid men or at least know to act loving to some extent before nuptials, however once they're married - they can then move into the controlling mode at a stronger rate. The boys grew up with their father who was not a spiritual leader and although they usually attended church regularly, he let his wife become the dominant leader spiritually. The boys' mother read her Bible most every day, read other spiritual books and was a good mother and wife while her husband only read his Bible occasionally, almost never cracked a spiritual book open, and was tired from working a full day. He wanted to relax when he got home or be involved in sports on the side with his friends as he wanted to stay away from his controlling wife.

Therefore, the same scenario is repeated in their children's lives as the spiritually passive son marries a spiritually strong woman. Thus, you become your father and see the same results that he did as the generational curse of living as a weak man of God is passed on from your grandfather to your father, to you and then eventually - your sons. There are familiar spirits that convince you that you just "aren't a strong spiritual leader" and that is how it is and there is nothing you can do about it. You take your family to church, but when it comes to spiritual things – that just isn't who you are. Since your father relinquished his proper role as spiritual leader to your mother and she tried as best she could to take it and run with it, you end up doing the exact same thing that he did. Surrendering your responsibility as spiritual leader to your wife because your mom took over for your dad is not acceptable, and most men know this if you ask them but do not know how to change themselves to become the leader they know God wants them to become.

The Bible states in 1 Corinthians 11:3 NKJV, "But I want you to know that the head of every man is Christ, the head of woman is man, and the head of Christ is God." Unfortunately, men are not taking their responsibility and this must change if we are going to see proper spiritual order restored in the body of Christ (and society around the world) as time is getting shorter for Christ's return to earth. It is time to stand up and to take back what the enemy has stolen from you because it is not the way the Lord has instructed.

If you ask most godly women – they really do not want to take the lead spiritually because they also know this is not what they are called to do. They want their husbands to lead, yet they also never saw their fathers lead spiritually so gravitate to what they are familiar with and know something must be done. If their husbands will not take charge, they must do it because someone needs to try to guide and direct the children. It becomes another vicious cycle of men marrying women like their mothers and women marrying men like their fathers; and this goes on and on for generation after generation after generation and the family unit becomes weaker and weaker as the enemy wins. Women will feel most secure when they know their husbands are following after the Lord and getting direction from God instead of doing their own thing based on their own fleshly desires or trying to make decisions on their own. Men will ultimately feel most connected to God and at peace when they are hearing Him direct them instead of relying on their wives who are not hearing the Lord for decisions or making their own decisions based on themselves. It is such a challenge and I have talked to many women over the years that want their husbands to lead and are pleading that they do so yet their husbands simply do not know how.

So if you grew up with a father who did not show you how to lead spiritually and then you marry a woman just like your mother who was closer to spiritual things, then the question is - how do you transform into the man you should be and transition your wife to allow you to lead and support you the way she was designed by the Lord? The older you are and the more that your mindsets have been set in place, the more challenging that will be for both of you but it can and should be pursued if you really want to live in marriage in the perfect design that the Lord has for you. It is never too late to do the right thing and start having a personal relationship with the Creator of the universe.

What I have seen is that once a man gets a taste of hearing from the Lord and seeing miracles in his life, he will be on fire for God quickly and his wife will become much closer to him because she is finally seeing him as the man of God she truly desires. The tremendous effects of the Holy Spirit are far more exciting to see than the regular day to day basic life that most are experiencing as a couple. It is like moving from a barren place in the desert to a lush meadow in the mountains as things start to come alive as the Lord will supernaturally bring you into a very real experience that nothing can replicate. It is a whole new adventure and that is what a man's soul really yearns for - to experience God in a way that is personal, hear His voice speak to him and give him direction, and to see the things that are spoken come to pass in his life.

When a man's wife sees that her husband is thirsting after the Lord, there is a new exciting intimacy that develops quickly between them and starts a fire inside of her because she no longer needs to try to lead the family as that is not the way the Lord programmed her. She wants to support her godly husband in the direction the Lord is taking him and then help him to accomplish what the Lord is telling him to do. It does not mean that your wife should simply stop trying to hear from the Lord though. Together, you should be on the same team and both hear from the Lord so that you can have a confirmation of various decisions and directions that the Lord would lead you both in. If your wife has led spiritually your entire marriage, it may be a little scary for her to give it up to you but it will ultimately be the best thing that ever happened to her and you. Before you know it, your wife will have a much stronger love for you than you ever could have realized, and all frustrations will fall off as you both change roles from what was not to be into what the Lord called you both to be. I have seen many marriages improve from suffering, strife, and ambivalence to amazing and on fire for God once the man starts to take his proper position in Christ and become interested in things from the Lord.

So while most men marry their mothers, so to say, they can take the healthy desires that drew them to their wives and modify the lack of spiritual requirements into what is strong for their relationship once they have determined in their minds that they will seek God in a new and powerful way. It is time to no longer be a momma's boy but to grow into the mighty man of valor that you were created by God to become. You can and must do it – as your life, your wife's life, and your children's lives depend upon it. Matthew 6:33 NKJV states, "But seek first the Kingdom of God and His righteousness, and all these things will be added to you." You must seek after the Lord and be righteous and pure before Him, and He will make things in your lives improve as you rest in the peace that you will feel from Him. Instead of worrying about your finances, children, wife, the economy, diseases, ISIS, etc., you can live every day in total peace because you will be able to rest trusting in the Lord every day.

CHAPTER 4

Excessive Control Takes Its Toll

The majority of men who attend church today are not operating in the fullness of who they are called to be in the Lord. They are not hearing the Lord direct them every day, are not praying for people, seeing them get healed, and are not providing prophetic words to people who need them to take them into their destiny in Christ. Most are simply going through the motions talking about surface issues: weather, stock market, the economy, or sports. Some may get together at men's events at church or "men summits" and then play games like cornhole, carpetball, horseshoes, frisbee, basketball, football, or perhaps go fishing and have campfires and bond. I know because I have been to many of them at several churches. Many men complain about having over-controlling and manipulative wives who do not allow them to try to lead their families or enjoy their lives (and of course many of the men are not equipped to lead spiritually to begin with). I feel like screaming at the top of my lungs to men to "wake up!" and get with the program and become who Christ called them to be – healthy spiritual leaders!

Many of these men (not all) marry women who take the lead spiritually because they are not doing what they are called to do because they never saw their father model it. Many of their wives become accustomed to telling them what to do. The men are usually nice guys who love the Lord, but many are married (not all) to women who were hurt through having either no father involvement in their lives due to busy work schedules, or fathers that were rejecting, controlling, harsh, and some even abusive to them. Thus, their wives have hearts that were hurt, and they learned they could not trust their fathers causing them to have to control all their circumstances out of fear. This causes them to be angry with their future husbands and take out all their pain on the ones that love them most. They feel they cannot trust any other man; so ultimately many (not all) partner with a spirit called Jezebel which tells them they need to control everything at an extreme level (and out of fear) or else it will not get done right. They tend to control their husbands excessively, not trusting him to lead or make key decisions for their family, and thus he feels even more beaten down and ultimately emasculated.

These women also tend to strive for key positions in the church and ministries so that they are looked up to by all and thus, battle to get into a position where they can make decisions over other people and where people will pat them on the back. The church and ministries often times have women who take over leading because other men have relinquished the responsibility that the Lord called them into. Understand I am not saying that all women who are leading in the church or ministry have the Jezebel spirit because most do not and are truly honest, pure, godly, and amazing women of God who desperately want to bring as many into the Kingdom as possible. You need to discern in the Spirit as to those with the Jezebel spirit as they will tend to gravitate to people with high positions in the church or ministries and try to become good friends with them so they can manipulate in order to obtain control and power. There just seems to be something not pure about them that is sometimes hard to put a finger on regarding exactly what is going on. Jezebel also often uses her sexuality to her advantage with men to make them feel good by touching their arms or resting their hands on their shoulders or arms when talking to them or asking to pray for them and touching them. Men can also operate in the Jezebel spirit if they had fathers who were excessively harsh and controlling. Many are pastors who will not allow people to utilize their giftings for fear of losing control and only trust a select few in their inner circle. You can learn much more about the Jezebel spirit by reading my book *Restored to Freedom* which has helped thousands of people gain freedom from the spirits of Jezebel and Leviathan, releasing them to behave in a pure and righteous manner both before the Lord and behind closed doors and ultimately - saving their marriages. The Lord told me that the Jezebel spirit is the number one spirit that causes divorce as well as church splits in the world.

When a woman is operating under the Jezebel spirit and controlling a man in excessive ways year after year, it takes a heavy toll on their relationship. Most times, it will cause them to ultimately meet with a counselor at their church or elsewhere, and if the counselor does not know how to spot the Jezebel spirit (which 95% do not nor has a clue about it), it is a waste of money and time on everyone's part (although the counselor may get paid). What will happen is that the woman will look and act innocent and pure before the counselor, and she will bring up some good points that her husband needs to work on but when they go back home, behind closed doors she will return to her either subtle or extreme controlling ways. Keep in mind that I have also worked with men who have the Jezebel spirit and they do the exact same thing because it is the same spirit within them so their tactics are all the same. If the wife has Jezebel, her husband will feel like he is going crazy because he will see that the striving starts when she speaks words that hurt him over and over and he can no longer stay silent so feels he must retaliate. That spirit will cause division between the husband and wife and normally separation will happen and ultimately, divorce. Jezebel is the nastiest spirit on earth and causes so much heartache in couples along with the Leviathan spirit (which is prideful, twists things, and blames instead of taking responsibility) so is very challenging to be freed from until the person is finally made aware that they are hosting them. It is possible that they could still deny they are affected by the spirits for months or longer until their lives become worse and they finally want total deliverance.

What needs to happen if one of the spouses suffers from the spirit of Jezebel and controls and manipulates the other the majority of the time? They need to take control of their lives, recognize that the spirit is affecting them, and then use their authority in Christ to command that spirit to go from them. I have powerful renunciation prayers that include the breaking of generational curses, the spirits of Jezebel, Leviathan, and Orion in my *Restored to Freedom* book and have seen many get instantly delivered because they no longer have a right to stay in that person to affect them anymore. It is a beautiful thing to watch as I have seen people on the verge of divorce on a Saturday who were scheduled to meet with an attorney the following Monday, whose spouse got delivered from Jezebel in less than an hour. They then cancelled their appointment on Monday and celebrated their 21st wedding anniversary a few months later. The challenge is to get people (primarily women) who have the Jezebel and Leviathan spirits to recognize that they have it and not deny it. That is why many have been mailing my *Restored To Freedom* book with no return address on it to their own spouse or others who they know are suffering from it. The Holy Spirit takes over in the privacy of their own homes and once they have it all explained and can understand what has been tormenting them for a lifetime, then it makes sense and they will then take their authority to command the spirits to go and the spirits will go. They are released and are restored to peace in their lives and they no longer speak controlling words, stop the manipulative behavior, and have a humble heart. Love, joy, and peace comes back into their lives, marriages, and ministry for the first time.

It is such a beautiful thing to see people who have been fighting and suffering for their entire lives finally understand what has been at the core the entire time and then gain freedom. It is truly a revelatory moment when a person finally can see what has been causing them to behave in fear, anxiety, anger, control, manipulation, and in sexually selfish ways. Once the spirits have left, they feel pure and righteous before the Lord and the heaviness of that spirit is no longer on them, so they feel lighter.

Once the Jezebel and Leviathan spirits are gone from one spouse, the other needs to be freed from the Ahab spirit because they are co-dependent on each other. It is time for the spiritually weak Ahab to change into the mighty man of valor that the Lord has called him to become. My next chapter goes into detail about who Ahab was in the Bible and how he abdicated his authority in the Lord to his wife Jezebel which caused an entire nation to falter and be decimated by evil. It is important to understand what happens spiritually when a man does not take his responsibility seriously and allows the enemy to circumvent the direction of the family. It is why our world is in the shape it is in today and needs to change. It is never too late to change and become who you really were created to be, and it really must be done so that when you stand before the Lord that he says "well done my good and faithful servant" instead of "well...." as then it will be too late.

Get ready to receive revelation of who Ahab was and what the spirit of Ahab is doing in today's society so you can recognize if you are operating in it yourself or in your own children (and others) to be able to help them change into a mighty warrior for the Lord instead of having the enemy dictate to you what he wants to do. 1 John 4:4 NKJV, "You are of God, little children, and have overcome them, because He who is in you is greater than he who is in the world." So stand up and in the words of the great Scottish freedom fighter

47

William Wallace (portrayed by Mel Gibson) in the 1995 movie *Braveheart* - yell out "FREEDOM!"

CHAPTER 5

Ahab Abdicates Authority

When a husband does not take his proper role in leading his wife or family spiritually, it greatly affects the entire structure of the family and allows the enemy to have free reign to hurt him, his wife, and his children. There is nothing more important than for a man to stand up and become a mighty man of valor and take his godly authority in Christ. It becomes a perpetual state of a downward spiral of Christ-like leadership in all of society when a generation of men abdicate their God commanded responsibility to lead spiritually and fail to train up their children as unto the Lord. What we are dealing with today is that the lion's share of men have relinquished their calling from the Lord and have given it to their wives, and many of them do not want to take it because they are not supposed to. It is important to understand a real-life story in the Bible of what happens when a man does not do what he is supposed to do in being directed by the Lord and instead - follows his own fleshly desires and allows his spouse (who does not serve the Lord) to rule. The man's name was Ahab.

"30 Now Ahab the son of Omri did evil in the sight of the Lord, more than all who were before him. 31 And it came to pass, as though it had been a trivial thing for him to walk in the sins of Jeroboam the son of Nebat, that he took as wife Jezebel the daughter of Ethbaal, king of the Sidonians; and he went and served Baal, and worshiped him."

I Kings 16:30-31

Ahab, son of Omri, the seventh king of Israel, reigned for twenty-two years, from 876 to 854, and was considered one of the most powerful yet also one of the weakest kings of Israel due to allowing his ungodly wife to control a nation.

The life of Ahab demonstrates principles in life that a man should never allow to become a part of his life. In other words, his life is a major example of what we as men should not want to become like, yet many today are doing that very thing. Ahab decided that the things that God advocated were considered inconsequential and of no concern instead of valuing the wisdom and admonition of the Lord. Ahab abdicated his spiritual authority instead of adhering to the Lord.

The ultimate goal of the spirit of Ahab is to destroy God's ordained authority and responsibility in the family and in the body of Christ as well as shutting down anyone who flows in prophetic giftings, deliverance from enemy spirits, or healing ministries. A spirit of Ahab symbolizes the abdicating of our authority in Christ and the excusing of godly responsibility. Does this sound like most churches today in the world? So many men that I have seen in the typical church (especially larger churches where they can just slip in and out without taking any responsibility or being held accountable) just go through the motions of trying to appear godly in front of their peers, yet never press into the Lord and actually hear His voice so they can be directed each and every day of their lives.

The Word of God teaches that the man is the head or spiritual authority of the woman, thus also the head or authority of his own home. He is not to behave in an unhealthy, dominate way of wielding improperly excessive control but to lead by example in a loving and Christ-like perspective, upholding everything that is pure and righteous in the Lord with godly wisdom on every decision that he makes. The Word also teaches that the pastor is the head or authority of the local church, thus it is important to follow a pastor who is pure and righteous before the Lord and of highest integrity who knows who they are in Christ and does not operate under an Ahab or Jezebel spirit. The Ahab spirit primarily affects men in an attempt to destroy the male and his role of authority and responsibility but can also be on a woman who marries a man who operates in Jezebel's controlling spirit.

Working together, the spirits of Ahab and Jezebel will stealthily form what is known as an unhealthy, twisted, codependent relationship. The Jezebel affected person will control and manipulate their Ahab spouse and the Ahab spouse will give up their spiritual authority in order to let many choices be determined by Jezebel because they typically have challenges making the tough decisions or standing up for what is righteous. They simply find it easier to yield to their spouse instead of fighting for what is the godly, righteous decision in order to keep the peace with their Jezebel spouse.

Many couples in the church today have one spouse that is affected by Jezebel and they will usually marry a person who exhibits the Ahab spirit so they can control them. About 60% of women suffer from the Jezebel spirit and 60% of men suffer from the Ahab spirit. Conversely 30% of men struggle with the Jezebel spirit and 30% of women with the Ahab spirit. Twice as many women suffer from Jezebel then men because women's hearts need to be treated more gently by their fathers and they cannot take rejection or harshness as easily as a man is able to. Also women are sexually violated twice as much as men (one study indicates about 50% of women are touched sexually by the time they are 18 years of age. It would make sense that those who are married to the Jezebel spirit will be affected by the Ahab spirit accordingly to some degree. If you have a church with 100 people in it, you may have 40 that suffer from Jezebel to some degree and then their spouses would usually suffer from the Ahab spirit.

Both Jezebel and Ahab will need to feed off each other in order to accomplish each one's goals. A pastor who is influenced by an Ahab spirit will need someone affected by a Jezebel spirit to maintain his position and enlarge or entrench his power base. It helps him to get more people to come to the church through Jezebel's promotional capabilities via her charismatic personality and persuasion. Jezebel appears to be so pure, loving, and alluring - but then there will be several imperceptible incidences of unhealthy control and manipulation that will rear her ugly head. Most every church and ministry in the world has people that attend it who suffer from the Jezebel and Ahab spirits and until they are helped to be delivered, the church will suffer greatly with the impurity associated in their lives and will afflict others in the church that are innocent.

King Ahab rekindled associations with the Phoenicians and locked them in by his marriage to Jezebel, daughter of Ethbaal, king of Tyre. This was in spite of warnings by God that the Israelites should not intermarry with idol worshipers. He purposely disobeyed the Lord and violated his covenant with God causing hundreds of the Lord's priests to die, and a nation to feel the full effects of Satan upon them through his wicked wife Jezebel.

"2 And when the Lord thy God shall deliver them before thee; thou shalt smite them, and utterly destroy them; thou shalt make no covenant with them, nor show mercy unto them. 3 Neither shalt thou make marriages with them; thy daughter thou shalt not give unto his son, nor his daughter shalt thou take unto thy son. 4 For they will turn away thy son from following me, that they may serve other gods:

so will the anger of the Lord be kindled against you, and destroy thee suddenly." Deuteronomy 7:2-4 KJV

King Ahab should have married an Israelite woman who loved the Lord in every way and worshipped Him but instead - held God's sacred marriage in disregard and married a Sidonian daughter of a king which was purely for political and power considerations. Ahab married Jezebel to enhance his position for selfish gain however his marriage to her proved to be a major contributing factor in the eventual fall of the Omride dynasty.

King Ahab left the things of God to his wife Jezebel and as a result, she led him into her pagan religion instead of him leading her to follow the one true and living God and standing up for all things righteous and pure before the Lord. He forsook the Lord and followed after Baal and the curse over all the land ensued causing torment and falling away from the good things of the Lord. King Ahab then reestablished relations with Judah and sealed this alliance with the marriage of his daughter, Athaliah - to the crown prince of Judah (King Jehoshaphat's son), Jehoram.

An individual with an Ahab spirit will often make treaties instead of relationships because their mind-set is desperate to avoid confrontation and they will deny fault or taking ownership. Someone with an Ahab spirit would rather make peace at any cost, even if it leads to making an unholy alliance. How can you have a truce with someone who is out to destroy you? It is impossible but someone with an Ahab spirit will always sacrifice the future good for immediate peace today because of his inability to stand up and do the right thing. He would rather avoid all confrontations and allow sin and evil to dictate instead of standing up for righteousness because it is harder and requires significant effort to accomplish.

The Ahab spirit causes a man to be indecisive, unstable, and weak spiritually in all his ways every day of his life. King Ahab was efficient and strong in manipulative and administrative powers, but was weak and wavering in the face of his powerful wife Jezebel because he did not want to deal with her when it came to confrontations because verbally - she would win at all costs and wear him down until he gave her what she wanted. If he gave in to her demands, he could retain a more peaceful atmosphere but if he challenged her - she would verbally berate him until he was worn out and finally gave in. Does this sound familiar to anyone reading this book? He ended up giving his authority as king to his wife and even when she abused it - he remained passive and avoided confrontation which ultimately let her have her own way to try to keep the peace. She was dominate and he simply did not stand up for what he knew was the right thing to do. He allowed sinful behavior to occur because it was too hard to stand up for what was right because he knew that he would suffer the wrath of Jezebel and endure a verbal battle. Does this sound like anyone that you know?

With the Ahab spirit, the wife wrestles away the head position of the home because the Ahab husband doesn't want it since it takes too much energy from him. He is not used to leading because he never saw his own father being a godly or spiritual leader of his home. Most people do not realize that if a home is out of order, God will allow it to come under a curse and that is why you are seeing such families in total disarray. Too many fathers, through rebellion, rejection, and lust - have not lived as a godly example to their wife and children. The end result of this neglect opens the door for rebellious spirits to enter his wife and children causing strife to proliferate. Too many men fail to provide spiritual leadership in their homes and too often, the spirit of Jezebel surfaces in the wife causing the wife to be given the headship of the home spiritually, which is not the design by God. This is a very serious part of the Ahab spirit at work.

Many children in a 'Babylonian' family (Ahab/Jezebel) take on the same characteristics as those of their parents and some of them become even worse.

Girls:

- Many become man-haters
- Aggressive
- Disrespectful
- Verbally militaristic
- Demanding
- Can be interested in covert witchcraft / demonic control either directly or unbeknownst to them as a means of gaining power and control over people
- Often involved in sexual promiscuity, sexual perversion, lesbianism, drugs and alcohol abuse to escape their pain.

Boys:

- Do not like confrontations
- Become weak spiritual leaders
- Strong desire to make everyone happy
- Self-centered and selfish
- Lazy and complacent
- A momma's boy
- Learn early to use women to get what they want
- Struggle with pornography if married to women with the spirit of Jezebel
- Afraid of being rejected
- Afraid of making the wrong decision
- Too nice of a person and can be taken advantage of
- Become cry-babies in order to get someone to feel sorry
- Typically involved in sexual promiscuity, pornography, sometimes homosexuality, drugs and alcohol abuse to escape their pain.

The main characteristics of the Ahab spirit are lack of desire to take responsibility for spiritual leadership and addressing issues that are challenging. It simply does not want to be bothered. It will cause the man to let his wife handle problems that he should be taking care of because he wants to avoid confrontation. This is an issue of transferring of responsibilities; and in doing this the man becomes weaker and weaker and may even feel worthless and inept. The Ahab spirit is a rejected and insecure individual, is subject to withdrawal and low self-esteem, and some also exhibit poor self-confidence and lack of spiritual conviction. As long as he has access to pornography or perhaps visits regularly to massage parlors or even prostitutes, he is content because he is getting his sexual needs fulfilled. When he can have his own selfish pleasures and pursuits of the world, his wife can do anything she wants. It is a life void of any true intimacy for both people and is very sad and depressing and ultimately - ends in divorce. I have seen many women that have Jezebel divorce their husbands if they feel they can no longer control them (their men separate from them hoping their desire for a healthy marriage is stronger than the spirit controlling them).

A man with an Ahab spirit usually believes there is a God, but it's just not worth the effort or time it takes to commit his life to the Lord in a strong and powerful way, especially since he never saw his own father modeling it before him as he grew up. He will abdicate his head position as priest of the family instead of leading like a true man of God. The wife is often the one that takes the kids to church every Sunday and attends meetings during the week as he pursues fleshly desires like hanging out with his friends, going fishing, watching sports, etc. He does not care and would rather not be bothered with taking on other responsibilities. His lusts for the flesh and the world are too great to give up and he is too interested in gratifying his own self-serving perverted desires.

With the Ahab spirit present, reading the Bible is not consistent and sometimes non-existent. He rarely prays with his family and may just periodically say the blessing at the table because he feels guilty for the sins he does in secret as the enemy condemns him and makes him feel entrapped with no hope for breaking out of his prison. He may even purposefully be gone or hide in the bedroom when church people come over to the house because the spirit in him feels convicted by the godly spirit in others. He makes up many excuses - from blaming the hypocrites in the church, to his need for rest from working all week, to just not fitting in. He may even encourage his wife to go to church by herself as it gets her out of his hair and gives him more time for his own selfish and sinful private delights.

If persuaded to show up in church, he does it begrudgingly with no desire other than to satisfy his "nagging" wife. He hangs back and if forced to engage in church affairs, he runs from leadership unless it involves having fun with the guys at a retreat that includes fishing, boating, playing cards, horseshoes, or any other sport of his fancy. The food also helps with attendance if they are providing bacon, steaks, or pie. With minimal effort, he will hardly be enthusiastic about church projects. Emptying the garbage can and mowing the grass are about the only responsibilities he wants.

The man with an Ahab spirit is not necessarily physically weak; he can be strong and athletic, desiring to stay in shape. In fact, he loves the human body. An Ahab spirit loves nudity and is an easy victim to pornography. After all, King Ahab was a warrior and he loved battle; it was a game to him. The man with the Ahab spirit often times loves sports and is very competitive. If he cannot participate, he loves to watch on TV or go to games.

Here are a few examples of how the Spirit of Ahab works:

1) Considers the things of God as being inconsequential
2) Does not have a healthy fear of the Lord toward sin and the effects it has on him
3) Dislikes using his God-given authority for decision making
4) Enjoys childish things, sulking, temper tantrums
5) May call his wife 'mom' or 'mama'
6) May want to act like a 'little boy' instead of a godly man

7) Usually attracted to a Jezebel-type wife, giving him excuses to commit adultery, get drunk, act irresponsibly, and rationalize situations

8) Views parenting as playing with the children, but avoiding the unpleasant duties of correcting or discipline

9) Puts 'being out with the boys' above his family duties

10) Doubts his own abilities because he is insecure in himself

11) Does not prioritize or value his marriage

12) Unable to cope with his wife's problems so tunes her out

13) Attempts to appease his Jezebel wife and avoid arguments by letting her have her way instead of addressing the issues and doing the right thing

14) Often has a 'competitive' spirit wanting to win at everything but also wanting to receive accolades and praise

15) People pleaser – doing what others want him to do to cause everyone to like him

16) Goals are wealth at any cost, success, status, greed, and being lifted on a pedestal

17) Can be a workaholic because this takes him away from family responsibilities and issues that could require confrontations

18) Does not want to lead but very critical of those who do

19) Passive for the most part but can be aggressive if pushed past the point of tolerance

20) Feels inadequate to support his family, gets frustrated, leaves the house

21) Struggles with lust, love of body, nudity, pornography, sexual-perversion, masturbation, adultery, sometimes homosexuality

22) Lazy, carelessness, irresponsible, manipulative

23) Insecure, rejection, self-centeredness, self-pity, unstable, avoids all confrontations

24) Had a father that suffered from Ahab spirit who modeled for him the same behavior which becomes a generational curse

25) Feelings of hopelessness because they can never change even though they know they need to become who they are supposed

to be in Christ and know that they need to be the spiritual leader of their home but cannot make themselves become who they are supposed to be

The Ahab spirit, rooted in the destruction of the family priesthood, causes a man to forsake his responsibilities as the head of the household. He not only refuses to take the spiritual headship, but sometimes will not take responsibility for working to make enough for the living expenses for his wife and children. A man is to provide both spiritual and material security for his family although the Lord may direct him in spiritual pursuits for a season but only if provision is able to be made to make available for their needs. If he chooses not to provide for his family's needs, he will usually have issues with God and there will be negative circumstances that will befall him. As the spiritual canopy of defense for his wife and children, he is charged with the difficult role of prophet and priest for them which is an awesome responsibility to have and one not to be taken lightly.

It is interesting to note that the Lord revealed to me that many men who struggle with pornography are influenced at a strong level by the Ahab spirit. What the Lord showed me was that because many of those men are married to women who have the Jezebel spirit afflicting them – their sexual lives are tainted and perverted due to the Jezebel spirit being present in their wives. In other words, a person with the Jezebel spirit does not have pure and loving sexual relations with her husband the way the Lord designed. Typically, they either limit sex to control their husband or they desire to have selfish sex and it's all about them having orgasms in a perverted way instead of a loving and pure way the Lord intends for every couple to experience. The woman with the Jezebel spirit unfortunately may cause her husband sexually to have an unhealthy temptation to move into pornography or masturbation which the enemy uses to put a wedge between them. No man truly wants to do this because it is impersonal and void of love in every way - especially men who attend church and go through a cycle of sinning and repenting over and over again as they feel tremendous guilt and shame. When the woman gets free from Jezebel and the man is free from Ahab, something most beautiful occurs. They will have the most pure and honorable sexual relationship that anyone could dream of and it is unlike any feeling both will have ever experienced. Jezebel is the driving spirit behind everything perverted sexually - ads on television, movies, fashion, all encouraging women to use their bodies to tempt men. It is time for men to stand up for what is righteous and pure and say enough is enough.

The classic example of a modern-day Ahab would be that of former president Bill Clinton. He was an admitted philanderer addicted to fulfilling his sexual needs through other women and, of course, his wife Hillary is a modern-day Jezebel if ever there was one. When you think about how Jezebel in the Bible killed Naboth because he would not sell his vineyard to Ahab in 1 Kings 21 and as of the writing of this book - over 90 people closely associated with the Clintons have mysteriously died (59 in plane crashes, 13 murders, 10 suicides, 4 Waco assaults and 3 accidents), there's a definite correlation that the Jezebel spirit is alive and well in today's world. Bill was president, but Hillary wanted the power that came with that position so she could accomplish all that she wanted. Bill was happy just to have his deviate sexual needs fulfilled by various women who he could utilize while allowing Hillary to maneuver her way into more political positions to attain her future desires of getting into the U.S. Senate, followed by presidential aspirations.

Therefore the Ahab spirit is alive and well in today's society and is undermining the godliness of our world due to men not taking their proper authority spiritually in the Lord. If you identify with the behaviors of the Ahab spirit, it is time to stand up and be counted and break free of this spirit.

If you remain an Ahab and your spouse a Jezebel, what just may happen to your own children? What happened to the children of Jezebel and Ahab? Athaliah, Ahaziah, and Jehoram are listed below and what their lives turned out to be.

Below is a very good overview of Athaliah from "All the women of the Bible" by Herbert Lockyer.

Athaliah: The Woman Who Was a Notorious Murderess

Scripture References—2 Kings 8:26; 11; 2 Chronicles 22; 23:13-21; 24:7

Name Meaning—Taken away of the Lord, or Jehovah has afflicted. Athaliah is also the name of two males (1 Chronicles 8:26, 27; Ezra 8:7).

Family Connections - She was the daughter of Ahab and Jezebel, and so was half Israelite and half Phoenician. She personified all the evil of her ill-famed parents and transferred the poison of idolatry into Jerusalem's veins. She was the granddaughter of Omri, 6th king of Israel, "who waded through slaughter to a throne he never inherited." Athaliah married Jehoram, son of Jehoshaphat. After many years of strife between the kingdoms of Judah and Israel, political relations were friendlier. As a father of political expediency on the part of Jehoshaphat—which remains a blot upon his otherwise good memory—he gave his eldest son, Jehoram, in marriage to Athaliah whose brothers, loyal to the worship of Jehovah were murdered by Jehoram. Of this union Ahaziah was born who, with such a revolting figure as a mother, licentious and the personification of despicable arrogance, never had a chance to develop finer qualities of character. With such a mother as his wicked counselor, what else could he do but walk in the ways of godless Ahab (2 Chronicles 22:3)

After reigning for eight years Jehoram died, unmourned, of a predicted incurable disease. While he reigned, he was dominated by Athaliah who had the stronger character of the two, and who, having inherited from her evil mother strength of will and fanatical devotion to the worship of Baal, made Judah idolatrous. Ahaziah only reigned for a year. Wounded in battle by Jehu, he fled to Megiddo, where he died, and his wicked mother (2 Chronicles 24:7) became envious of the throne. But the sons of Ahaziah stood in her way, and with fanatical ambition she seized the opportunity and massacred all the legal heirs—so she thought. This wholesale, merciless, cruel-hearted murderess sought to exterminate the last vestiges of the House of David through which the promised Messiah was to come. Behind her dastardly crime to destroy "The Seed Royal" we can detect the evil machinations of the devil—a murderer from the beginning—to annihilate the promised seed of the woman predestined to bruise the satanic head. A bad woman bent on destruction is doubly dangerous.

After putting to death her young grandsons, Athaliah reigned for six years, and was the only woman to reign as queen of Judah. The daughter of a king, wife of a king and mother of a king, she is now queen. While her husband reigned, she was the power behind the throne—now she is the power on the throne, and proof of her energy, forcefulness and ability are seen in the length of her reign. A despotic ruler, her every gesture had to be obeyed. During her reign, part of the Temple of Jehovah was pulled down and the material used in the building of a temple of Baal. But the God who over-rules in the destinies of men and nations, intervened to redeem His promise of a Saviour from the tribe of Judah.

Unknown to Athaliah as she set out to massacre all her grandsons, the youngest was hid from the orgy of destruction. The sister of Ahaziah, Jehosheba, wife of Jehoiada the high priest hid Joash until he was seven years old (2 Kings 11:2; 2 Chronicles 22:11). Jehoiada had plotted to put Joash (Jehoash) on the throne and waited for the opportune moment to declare the remaining son of Ahaziah the lawful king of Judah.

Athaliah came into the Temple as the coronation of Joash took place, and rending her robe, cried, "Treason!" To save the Temple from being defiled with her evil blood she was slain just outside the door where the avenging guards waited to end her infamous life. Thus, as Edith Deen expresses it, "The horses trampled over her body where she lay dead at the gates. In her miserable end, Athaliah bore a singular resemblance to her mother Jezebel, who was abandoned to the dogs. Athaliah was left in a horse-path, to be trampled upon. Like her mother, she died a queen but without a hand to help her or an eye to pity her."

Among the lessons one can gather from the record of this murderess is that we reap what we sow. To Athaliah life was cheap, and thus those who thwarted her purpose must be destroyed. But taking the sword, she perished by it. She breathed out murder and was in turn murdered. A further lesson we learn from her stained history is that no one can thwart God's purposes of grace. Having promised a sinful world a Saviour, none could make such a promise null and void. Persecution and martyrdom have never been able to destroy the loyal worship of the true God. Idolatry and infidelity cannot possibly annihilate the imperishable Word of God. As we leave the shameful story of Athaliah, we find ourselves in full agreement with the summary of her bloody career as given by Dr. Robert G. Lee—

"Her very name is an execration. She put the whole nation under the shadow of a great horror. She trampled on all faith. She violated all obligations. She lived with the shrieks of those she butchered in her ears. She lived with her hands red with the blood of princes and princesses. She died, frantic with rage, with the accusation of treason on her lips. She died in the barnyard under the battleaxes of an aroused people."

Jehoram

Jehoram, or Joram, King of Israel

Jehoram was the son of Ahab and Jezebel. He was the ninth King of the northern kingdom of Israel. (There was also another man named Jehoram who became king of Judah. In fact, the Jehoram of Judah married the sister, Athaliah, of Jehoram of Israel). Jehoram succeeded his brother, Ahaziah, and reigned for twelve years.

He aligned himself with King Jehoshaphat of Judah to put down the Moabite rebellion. With a miracle as predicted by Elisha the prophet, the Moabites were defeated. Jehoram continued the long conflict between Israel and the nation of Aram.

After he was wounded at Ramoth Gilead, he went to the town of Jezreel to recover. While recovering, Jehu (who was anointed to be the next King of Israel), tracked down and killed Jehoram and became the next King of Israel. The story of Jehoram is found in 2 Kings.

The name Jehoram means "Yah is high."

Ahaziah

AHAZIAH (ā'ha-zī'a, Heb. 'ăhazyâh, Jehovah hath grasped)

Son of Ahab and Jezebel, eighth king of Israel. He reigned only briefly, 851-850 b.c. Ahaziah was a worshiper of Jeroboam's calves and of his mother's idols, Baal and Ashtoreth. The most notable event of his reign was the revolt of the Moabites, who had been giving a yearly tribute of a hundred thousand lambs and a hundred thousand rams (2 Kings 1:1; 2 Kings 3:4 2 Kings 3:5). Ahaziah was prevented from trying to put down the revolt by a fall through a lattice in his palace at Samaria. Injured severely, he sent messengers to inquire of Baalzebub, god of Ekron, whether he would recover. Elijah the prophet was sent by God to intercept the messengers and proclaimed to them that Ahaziah would die. The king in anger tried to capture the prophet, but two groups of fifty men were consumed by fire from heaven in making the attempt. A third contingent was sent to seize the prophet but instead - implored Elijah to deliver them from the fate of their predecessors (2 Kings 1:13, 2 Kings 1:14). Elijah then went down to Samaria and gave the message directly to the king, who died shortly afterward. He was succeeded by his brother Jehoram (2 Kings 1:17; cf. 2 Kings 8:16). Son of Jehoram of Judah and Athaliah; thus, grandson of Jehoshaphat and Ahab, and nephew of Ahaziah of Israel. He was the sixth king of Judah in the divided monarchy and reigned only one year (2 Chr.22:2), 843 b.c. In 2 Chr.21:17 and 2 Chr.25:23, his name appears also as Jehoahaz (a simple changing of the names), and in 2 Chr.22:6 (KJV) he is called Azariah. According to 2 Kings 8:26, Ahaziah was twenty-two years old when he began to reign, and his father, Jehoram, only lived to age forty (2 Kings 21:20). However, 2 Chr.22:2 states that he was forty-two years old when he ascended the throne. Ahaziah walked in all the idolizations of the house of Ahab, "for his mother encouraged him in doing wrong" (2 Chr.22:3). He sinned also in allying himself with Joram (KJV "Jehoram") of Israel against Hazael of Syria, going into battle at Ramoth Gilead (2 Chr.22:5). Joram was wounded and Ahaziah went to see him at Jezreel. Here judgment came on him through the hand of Jehu, who fell on Joram and all the house of Ahab. When Ahaziah saw the slaughter, he fled, but "they wounded him in his chariot...he escaped to Megiddo and died there" (2 Kings 9:27). The account given in Chronicles presents different though not irreconcilable details of his death (2 Chr.22:6, 2Chr.22:9). Ahaziah was buried with his fathers in Jerusalem (2 Kings 9:28). Jehu allowed this honorable burial because

Ahaziah was the grandson of Jehoshaphat, who sought the Lord with all his heart (2 Chr.22:9). Following the death of Ahaziah, his mother Athaliah seized the throne. She killed all the royal sons of the house of Judah except Joash, Ahaziah's son, who was hidden by Jehosheba, sister of Ahaziah and wife of Jehoiada the high priest (2 Chr.22:10-2 Chr.22:12).

So as you can see, the children who live under parents who are operating in the Jezebel and Ahab spirits do not typically have a very good outcome as they usually will suffer greatly for their parents' ungodly behavior. Often times, the children will suffer with divorces and much physical sickness and infirmities unless the cycle is broken, and that is why it is so extremely important for a man to take a spiritual stand and break off the cycle of the Ahab spirit in his life so that he can change what the enemy has meant for evil in his life and the lives of his children and become a true man of God. Ahabs generally will gravitate towards marrying Jezebel women and vice versa. If an Ahab spirit affected man is divorced from his Jezebel wife, he will unknowingly continue to seek out strong willed Jezebel-type women in the future and his misery will continue to perpetuate over a lifetime. It is time for the men in this world to take a stand for righteousness and purity and be mighty men of valor. It will take effort, but it will be worth it as you become one with the Father who created you. There is nothing more satisfying for a man to reach the destiny and life purpose of the One that created him.

CHAPTER 6

Who Did God Say You Are?

When attempting to break free from a lifetime of weak spiritual authority - it is important to know who God says you are and how you should live your life in Him. Since you never saw your father model behavior that exhibited hearing the voice of the Lord and living in purity and righteousness as well as being bold and confident in the Lord, it is so important to get into your spirit exactly who you really are supposed to be as a strong man of God. Just how do you transform yourself from being ineffective in your current walk to a powerful lion in the Spirit that the Lord has called you to be? To start, it is important to read scriptures that tell you who you really are in Christ as this will help your spirit to get excited inside as it hears about how you can transform into the man of God that the Father created you to be and that which is your destiny.

The following scriptures will help you better understand your true calling as a powerful man or woman of Christ and provide you with hope for the changes that need to take place that will come to pass if you commit yourself to it for a lifetime. I know, first-hand, what it is like to just go through the motions (not have a personal relationship with Christ, never hear from the Lord, never see any miracles) and then be transformed and see amazing miracles, signs and wonders, and help others become who they are in Christ. I will never be the same again and know that if God did it for me, He will definitely do it for you because He loves you and wants a personal relationship with all of His people. There is nothing in the world like actually hearing from the Lord whenever you need insight or wisdom on a situation. The Lord wants to speak to you and give you guidance and wisdom from above.

Free from Indwelling Sin

Romans 8:1-39 NKJV,

"[1]There is therefore now no condemnation to those who are in Christ Jesus, who do not walk according to the flesh, but according to the Spirit. [2] For the law of the Spirit of life in Christ Jesus has made me free from the law of sin and death. [3] For what the law could not do in that it was weak through the flesh, God did by sending His own Son in the likeness of sinful flesh, on account of sin: He condemned sin in the flesh, [4] that the righteous requirement of the law might be fulfilled in us who do not walk according to the flesh but according to the Spirit. [5] For those who live according to the flesh set their minds on the things of the flesh, but those who live according to the Spirit, the things of the Spirit. [6] For to be carnally minded is death, but to be spiritually minded is life and peace. [7] Because the carnal mind is enmity against God; for it is not subject to the law of God, nor indeed can be. [8] So then, those who are in the flesh cannot please God.

"9 But you are not in the flesh but in the Spirit, if indeed the Spirit of God dwells in you. Now if anyone does not have the Spirit of Christ, he is not His. 10 And if Christ is in you, the body is dead because of sin, but the Spirit is life because of righteousness. 11 But if the Spirit of Him who raised Jesus from the dead dwells in you, He who raised Christ from the dead will also give life to your mortal bodies through His Spirit who dwells in you."

Sonship Through the Spirit

"12 Therefore, brethren, we are debtors—not to the flesh, to live according to the flesh. 13 For if you live according to the flesh you will die; but if by the Spirit you put to death the deeds of the body, you will live. 14 For as many as are led by the Spirit of God, these are sons of God. 15 For you did not receive the spirit of bondage again to fear, but you received the Spirit of adoption by whom we cry out, "Abba, Father." 16 The Spirit Himself bears witness with our spirit that we are children of God, 17 and if children, then heirs—heirs of God and joint heirs with Christ, if indeed we suffer with Him, that we may also be glorified together."

From Suffering to Glory

"18 For I consider that the sufferings of this present time are not worthy to be compared with the glory which shall be revealed in us. 19 For the earnest expectation of the creation eagerly waits for the revealing of the sons of God. 20 For the creation was subjected to futility, not willingly, but because of Him who subjected it in hope; 21 because the creation itself also will be delivered from the bondage of corruption into the glorious liberty of the children of God. 22 For we know that the whole creation groans and labors with birth pangs together until now. 23 Not only that, but we also who have the firstfruits of the Spirit, even we ourselves groan within ourselves, eagerly waiting for the adoption, the redemption of our body. [24] For we were saved in this hope, but hope that is seen is not hope; for why does one still hope for what he sees? [25] But if we hope for what we do not see, we eagerly wait for it with perseverance.

"[26] Likewise the Spirit also helps in our weaknesses. For we do not know what we should pray for as we ought, but the Spirit Himself makes intercession for us with groanings which cannot be uttered. [27] Now He who searches the hearts knows what the mind of the Spirit is, because He makes intercession for the saints according to the will of God.

"[28] And we know that all things work together for good to those who love God, to those who are the called according to His purpose. [29] For whom He foreknew, He also predestined to be conformed to the image of His Son, that He might be the firstborn among many brethren. [30] Moreover whom He predestined, these He also called; whom He called, these He also justified; and whom He justified, these He also glorified."

God's Everlasting Love

"[31] What then shall we say to these things? If God is for us, who can be against us? [32] He who did not spare His own Son, but delivered Him up for us all, how shall He not with Him also freely give us all things? [33] Who shall bring a charge against God's elect? It is God who justifies. [34] Who is he who condemns? It is Christ who died, and furthermore is also risen, who is even at the right hand of God, who also makes intercession for us. [35] Who shall separate us from the love of Christ? Shall tribulation, or distress, or persecution, or famine, or nakedness, or peril, or sword? [36] As it is written:

'For Your sake we are killed all day long;
We are accounted as sheep for the slaughter.'

"37 Yet in all these things we are more than conquerors through Him who loved us. 38 For I am persuaded that neither death nor life, nor angels nor principalities nor powers, nor things present nor things to come, 39 nor height nor depth, nor any other created thing, shall be able to separate us from the love of God which is in Christ Jesus our Lord."

You are to walk every day in the spirit and not the flesh. The flesh wants you to sin, but your spirit wants you to serve the Lord and be blessed with Heavenly gifts from above all your days instead of having your blessings blocked by sin. You are more than a conqueror when you are in the spirit. God loves you so much and wants you to talk with Him every day (and in the evenings He wants to give you prophetic dreams showing you the future that He has for you). God wants to bless His people but can only do so when we align our will with His; because otherwise it can cause us to move farther away from Him if we sin on a regular basis. That gives the enemy a toe hold and a right to harm us and blocks the blessing from the Lord.

1 John 4:4 NKJV,

"You are of God, little children, and have overcome them: because He who is in you is greater than he who is in the world."

What does this mean? Since you have given your life to Christ, it is important to recognize that Christ is greater than the enemy in the world. Christ trumps Satan every time and therefore, if Christ defeated Satan and Christ lives in you - you can trump Satan as well. You just need to get that revelation into your spirit and walk in it every day.

Romans 7:15-19 NKJV,

"15 For what I am doing, I do not understand. For what I will to do, that I do not practice; but what I hate, that I do. 16 If, then, I do what I will not to do, I agree with the law that it is good. 17 But now, it is no longer I who do it, but sin that dwells in me. 18 For I know that in me (that is, in my flesh) nothing good dwells; for to will is present with me, but how to perform what is good I do not find. 19 For the good that I will to do, I do not do; but the evil I will not to do, that I practice."

Understand that when you are not close to the Lord that your flesh makes many decisions for you and will cause you to sin, giving the enemy a right to come in and hurt you and draw you further away from your authority in Christ. When you are pursuing the things of the spirit, your desires will become more like Christ and your desire to sin will fall off. Think of things that are pure and righteous every day and watch how the enemy will no longer have control over your every thought anymore.

Ephesians 6:12 NKJV,

"For we do not wrestle against flesh and blood, but against principalities, against powers, against the rulers of the darkness of this age, against spiritual hosts of wickedness in the heavenly places."

This battle that you are in every day to do what is right in the Lord is one that is real and is in the spirit world. The Jezebel spirit wants to shut down the ability of a man or woman to become who they are in Christ and not be able to minister effectively and set people free. Press in to the Lord every day and do not give up – be who you really are in Christ. The Ahab spirit also wants to keep you from operating in the full strength of the Lord. Do not give up but press forward every day.

Philippians 4:13NKJV,

"I can do all things through Christ who strengthens me."

What things can you do through Christ? All things. What is the definition of all? Everything, the whole, entire, total amount, every member or part of. All means all. Therefore, you can stand up and step out and be bold and confident in who you are in Christ. The enemy must bow to you, not the other way around. Speak life and boldness over yourself because when you speak out loud who you really are in Christ, you will eventually change into that person as you will be prophesying your future.

The Whole Armor of God

Ephesians 6:10-20 NJKV,

"[10] Finally, my brethren, be strong in the Lord and in the power of His might. [11] Put on the whole armor of God, that you may be able to stand against the wiles of the devil. [12] For we do not wrestle against flesh and blood, but against principalities, against powers, against the rulers of the darkness of this age, against spiritual hosts of wickedness in the heavenly places. [13] Therefore take up the whole armor of God, that you may be able to withstand in the evil day, and having done all, to stand.

"[14] Stand therefore, having girded your waist with truth, having put on the breastplate of righteousness, [15] and having shod your feet with the preparation of the gospel of peace; [16] above all, taking the shield of faith with which you will be able to quench all the fiery darts of the wicked one. [17] And take the helmet of salvation, and the sword of the Spirit, which is the word of God; [18] praying always with all prayer and supplication in the Spirit, being watchful to this end with all perseverance and supplication for all the saints— [19] and for me, that utterance may be given to me, that I may open my mouth boldly to make known the mystery of the gospel, [20] for which I am an ambassador in chains; that in it I may speak boldly, as I ought to speak."

These verses explain how we battle the enemy in the spirit by learning who we are in Christ. As you transform into who you really are from who you were, you will have such boldness to speak to the enemy that nothing will be able to thwart you from being who you were born to be. See yourself with a powerful sword cutting the enemy in half and taking out every demonic force that has tried to keep you from your destiny. So much of the Word is to teach us about who we are when we have Christ in us. It changes everything in our lives once we come into who we are in the Lord.

Our Compassionate High Priest

Hebrews 4:14-16 NKJV,

"[14] Seeing then that we have a great High Priest who has passed through the heavens, Jesus the Son of God, let us hold fast our confession. [15] For we do not have a High Priest who cannot sympathize with our weaknesses, but was in all points tempted as we are, yet without sin. [16] Let us therefore come boldly to the throne of grace, that we may obtain mercy and find grace to help in time of need."

We are to be bold in all our ways – not wimpy or complacent. Jesus was tempted in all the ways we were yet was able to not sin. As you become more like Christ every day, you will also lose desire to blatantly sin as it will become repugnant to whom you are in Christ. It may be hard to believe because you have been operating in the old sin nature of man, but as you press in and spend time hearing the Lord speak to you - then you will dramatically transform into who you really are in Christ. The ephemeral things of the flesh and this world will seem like such a waste of time to pursue anymore and you will desire all of Christ because of the amazing power and authority to change others' lives to become more like Christ. Greater is He that is in you than he that is in the world!

Living Sacrifices to God

Romans 12 NKJV,

"[1] I beseech you therefore, brethren, by the mercies of God, that you present your bodies as a living sacrifice, holy, acceptable to God, which is your reasonable service. [2] And do not be conformed to this world, but be transformed by the renewing of your mind, that you may prove what is that good and acceptable and perfect will of God."

As you become more like Christ, you will lose your desire to sin as there will be no more appeal for it. I have seen it in my own life as I became more excited about experiencing things of the Lord such as hearing Him speak to me (in my head), seeing miracles, signs and wonders in those who I prayed for, and the desire to sin just fell off of me. As you become more like Christ and hear from the Lord, you want nothing to do with the enemy's ways and plans or vices. Sin becomes repulsive because that is not who you are anymore. Your spirit desires to be pure and righteous before the Lord; so as you transition to the more godly lifestyle - you will be excited every day to see what the Lord does to unite you with His people through divine connections, learn more about how to hear the voice of the Lord and how to love on others like Christ, and the things of this world will hold no interest for you anymore.

Meditate on These Things

Philippians 4:8-9 NKJV,

"8 Finally, brethren, whatever things are true, whatever things are noble, whatever things are just, whatever things are pure, whatever things are lovely, whatever things are of good report, if there is any virtue and if there is anything praiseworthy—meditate on these things. 9 The things which you learned and received and heard and saw in me, these do, and the God of peace will be with you."

When the enemy is afflicting you, then you could feel angry, vindictive, anxious, worried, fearful, lustful, etc., but when you are thinking on things from the Lord such as things that are truthful, noble, just, pure, lovely, good, virtuous, and praising the Lord, then you will have the peace of God in your life. I used to have over $500,000 for my net worth but did not have peace because of what the enemy was doing to my family. I told the Lord I would give it all up if only I could have peace. The Lord told me He would do exactly that and within a few years I had no money left yet had more peace than I'd ever had on a day to day basis because I trusted in the Lord to meet all my needs every day. It was wonderful!

Striving to "keep up with the Joneses" is not what you want to do. Keeping up with Jesus is exactly what you want to do because then you will have peace and can sleep at night. If every day you complain, gripe, argue, fight, have anxiety and fear – you will eventually wear out and develop various sicknesses and infirmities. It is much better to become like Christ and walk every day in His peace, not worried about anything. The Lord told me that He would eventually bless me with exceedingly greater finances than I had before, but He would do it His way so that money did not own me but that I owned and controlled money for His purpose. In other words, I would use money for Kingdom purposes and use some for myself to enjoy but my heart has been transformed to serve Him and my family. Instead of working to live without knowing Christ in a personal way and not leading my wife and family spiritually, I now have the complete desire to grow closer to the Lord daily. My heart has changed and I am now doing ministry every day, and the Lord is blessing me with donations, book revenues, opportunities to minister at churches, conferences, retreats, etc., and I am loving every minute of it because I am helping people get freed from their past and launching them into their own destinies in Christ as well as their own ministries.

Joshua 1:9 NKJV,

"Have I not commanded you? Be strong and of good courage; do not be afraid, nor be dismayed, for the Lord your God is with you wherever you go."

Many men (and some women) are weak and afraid in the Lord because they do not know who they are in Christ nor have been taught their authority nor have a clue what it is like to be strong in the Lord. You are to be strong and courageous, and if you are not, then it is the enemy that is the author of all fear and worry. As you transition to becoming who you are in Christ, the enemy's hold on you will lessen and eventually you will have no fear as you learn your authority in Christ. My book *Jesus Loves To Heal Through You* explains in detail how we have the authority to command healing in our own bodies and in others in Jesus' name. When we pray like Jesus taught instead of like most everyone else in the world, then you will see miracles.

Judges 6:12 NKJV,

"And the Angel of the Lord appeared to him, and said to him, 'The Lord is with you, you mighty man of valor!'"

The Lord called Gideon a mighty man of valor. What does the term mean that you are a mighty man of valor? Mighty means having or showing great power, skill, strength, or force, imposing or awesome in size, degree, or extent: a mighty stone fortress. Valor means boldness or determination in facing great danger, especially in battle: heroic courage; bravery. Who would not want to be called a mighty man of valor by God? Everything in a man cries out for this signature to be bestowed upon him.

It is important to study the life of Gideon to more completely understand what it takes to become a mighty man of valor. The account of Gideon's life is recorded in Judges 6:11-8:32. The setting for Gideon's life begins with the Israelites being harmed by the Midianites as a result of their disobedience to God (Judges 6:1). For seven years they faced invasions from the mighty Midianites, Amalekites, and Eastern foreigners who ruined their crops and destroyed their cattle. Although they had been unfaithful to God by worshipping the gods of the Amorites, they cried out to God for His relief without realizing why this was happening to them (Judges 6:6). God sent them a prophet to remind them of how the one true and living God had provided for them in the past, and yet how quickly they had forgotten Him (Judges 6:8-10).

God heard their cries and kindly intervened by sending an angel to Gideon to call him into action (Judges 6:11-14). Gideon, whose name means "cutter" or "cutter of trees," belonged to a common family of the Abiezrites, but from the angel's connection we can assume that Gideon had already demonstrated what it was like to be a mighty warrior (Judges 6:12). Though Gideon was a willing servant of God, he needed assurance that it was, in fact, God calling him to this divine service (vs.17). In accomplishing the mission set before him by God, Gideon proved himself to be faithful and a mighty warrior, a strong leader of men (Judges 7:17), and a diplomat (Judges 8:1-3). As such, he was included in a fitting testimonial for the great men of faith in Hebrews 11:32-34. Just think what that tribute would have meant to you to be included in the Bible as one of the greatest men of faith. Instead of looking at yourself as a weakling in the order of faith - if you could see yourself as God sees you (as a mighty man of valor), then there is nothing you could not accomplish. Gideon was the fifth judge and renowned as the greatest of Israel.

The highlights of Gideon's life included his victorious battle against Israel's enemies. Nevertheless, we must not overlook his amazing faith, by which he carried out God's mission and which was first put to the test and confirmed when he destroyed the Baal idols that his father and the community had been worshipping (Judges 6:25-27). Can you imagine the fortitude that it took for Gideon to destroy what his father had set up? That is the kind of men that we need more of today. Gideon's battle triumph was preceded by God's anointing (Judges 6:34). When God calls you to step up your faith game, it is time to devote your life to Him. It is so worth it and you will never be disappointed. It was significant that Gideon managed to enlist his tribesmen, the Abiezerites, to go into battle with him. These were the men whose idols he had just destroyed and who had renamed him "Jerub-baal" (Judges 6:32). Before entering the battle, Gideon's troops numbered 32,000, but in obedience to God he reduced them by 22,000 (Judges 7:2-3)! Can you imagine getting ready to go into war with a mighty foe and dropping your numbers of soldiers by 67%! Again, and in obedience to God, he decreased the remaining 10,000 by a further 9,700, leaving him with just 300 men (vss. 7-8) – a full 99% reduction in their original force! This was against an enemy that is described as "thick as locusts" with "camels as numerous as the grains of sand on the seashore" (Judges 7:12). With the battle finally won, the people requested that Gideon rule over them as their king, but he declined their praises and tells them the Lord will rule over them (Judges 8:22-23). What a mighty man of valor, indeed.

Gideon had proved his faithfulness to God, and his obedience had required him to take a stand against his own father and tribe. Though he feared his own people (Judges 6:24), from the three requests he made for the Lord's confirmation of His will, it was evident he feared God much more. How many of you fear the Lord more than you do a human being? It is critical to hear the Lord's voice and then do exactly what He says regardless of those who influence your decisions that are not hearing from the Lord. It is far better to do what the Lord says and be ridiculed by men than to obey men and ignore what the Lord wants you to do. The Lord had called several men to have an amazingly anointed healing ministry, but all rejected the call so the Lord asked Kathryn Kuhlman. She said yes, and over her ministry life - healed over 1.5 million people!

In battle, Gideon took on far greater odds than were realistic to mere mortals. When the Israelites wanted to honor him as their king for triumphing over their enemies and restoring Israel's pride, Gideon recognized God as the real victor in the battle. He declined their request and gave the rightful sovereignty to God. This was a great test of Gideon's faithfulness when he could so easily have submitted to pride by accepting the people's honor. It is with amazing wonder that we see Gideon go on to compromise his faith by requesting they all contribute gold from the plunder of the battle, so he could create an "ephod," a breastplate or mask used in cultic worship (Judges 8:24-26). As we see in verse 27, it became a snare to Gideon and his family.

From Gideon's example, we can learn that no matter how great the odds against us may be - our faithful God is sovereign. He will always see us through whatever battles we face in life if we remain faithful to His calling and obedient to His commands. "Trust the Lord with all your heart and lean not on your own understanding; in all your ways acknowledge Him, and He will make your paths straight" (Proverbs 3:5-6). We can also see how God uses ordinary people to accomplish His plans, although with Gideon - the key factor was his willingness to obey God.

Sometimes, the most difficult people to witness our faith to are our families. The reason for that is because they have known us our entire lives and do not want to listen to us and do not respect what we have learned in Christ. We can see after Gideon destroys the false gods his family had been worshipping that he receives an anointing from the Lord. It was because of this anointing that he was able to accomplish the mission that God had set before him and it is with

God's anointing on our lives that we can truly claim "I can do all things through Him who gives me strength" (Philippians 4:13). Gideon had gone from being a warrior in hiding, threshing wheat at the foot of a hill out of sight of the enemy, to defeating the same enemy in battle. He was careful to ensure that it was God's will he was obeying. As the Apostle Paul wrote, "Do not conform any longer to the pattern of this world, but be transformed by the renewing of your mind. Then you will be able to test and approve what God's will is — his good, pleasing and perfect will" (Romans 12:2).

However, unlike Gideon, who had proved his faithfulness to God and received God's answers to his requested signs as an encouragement, we must not expect God to do likewise for those who request signs from God because of their doubts or weak faith. There may be times when everyone around us lacks the faith to go on, so it is up to us (like Gideon), to take the lead by our example and encourage the weak among us (Judges 7:17; Romans 15:1). Could you stand up to your friends or family that are not hearing God and do the opposite of what they want you to do? It is not an easy task to do what you know is the Lord's desires and receive tremendous verbal assaults and mockings from family and friends. That is exactly what the enemy wants to do to you – to keep you down and in fear of what others will say so that you are not able to accomplish what the Lord is directing.

It is important to do exactly what the Lord is directing you to do in order to accomplish the amazing transformation that He wants for you and the incredible miracles that He wants to do through you. When you begin to realize that you were created to be a mighty man of God and then speak it out of your mouth every day – then you will be able to see the manifestations of that very thing before your eyes over time. Press in and do not give up. Victory is yours!

CHAPTER 7

Breaking Free From The Past

When a person has lived in spiritual defeat their entire lives and is used to operating in the same weakened way every day for 30, 40, 50 or more years - how do you break free from the usual and become someone extraordinary in Christ? It is important to look back and understand (from a spiritual standpoint) just what went on in our lives to cause us to behave the way we do today. Once we have our spiritual eyes opened to the truth, that can help us to see how the enemy deceived us and caused us to get off track in order to break free from the past.

Recognize that your father, your father's father, and so forth and so on - behaved the way they did because of generations prior to them not taking their spiritual authority and devoting the time necessary to spend personally with the Lord. How can a father who does not keep close to the Lord affect his grandson or great grandson? It is important to review what the Bible says about this.

Exodus 20:5-6 NKJV,

" [5] you shall not bow down to them nor serve them. For I, the Lord your God, am a jealous God, visiting the iniquity of the fathers upon the children to the third and fourth generations of those who hate Me, [6] but showing mercy to thousands, to those who love Me and keep My commandments."

The above is talking about the Ten Commandments given to Moses for the Israelites to live by. Today, we are still expected by the Lord to adhere to the Commandments or else they would have been known as the Ten Suggestions. What does the word 'iniquity' really mean? It means immoral or grossly unfair behavior, wickedness, sinfulness, immorality, and impropriety. Basically, it means bad stuff that the Lord does not approve of. If we choose to willingly sin (whether it is known to other people or hidden, it is known by God), we are bringing a curse down our bloodlines to our children, grandchildren, and great grandchildren. We are then responsible for hurting our own family and descendants.

A key, real life example of this is how I have seen so many people that have visited my Healing Rooms at New Life Assembly of God in Noblesville who were experiencing pain in their backs, necks, tension, even cancer, etc., whose fathers, great-grandfathers, or even great, great grandfathers on either side of their parents that were involved in Freemasons, Scottish Rite, or Shriners. After researching this, I learned that they make oaths and pledges to the Great Architect of the Universe which is Satan instead of God and to Allah instead of Jesus. This opens up the door to bring a curse upon their lives and their loved ones, and invariably - people suffer from back and neck pain, scoliosis, headaches, migraines, cancer, and other maladies due to the right that the spirit of Leviathan from Job chapter 41 has to attack them. Unless and until they recognize what is attacking them, the spirit stays on them and can cause death.

In June of 2016, I appeared on The Harvest Show (on LeSea Broadcasting in South Bend, IN) to discuss my book *Jesus Loves to Heal Through You* and a lady from Minnesota just happened to turn it on that evening as it was rebroadcast. I prayed before I went on the show that the Lord would cause those that He wanted to see the show to just happen to turn it on at the right time when I was talking. Her sister was dying from 4th stage lung cancer and they wanted me to pray for her. When I got her on the phone, I sensed there was a spirit that was on her causing the cancer so I felt led to tell them about the Leviathan spirit that causes severe pain and disease (and often times cancer) and how it can come upon someone if anyone in the family was involved in Freemasonry, Scottish Rite, or Shriners. The lady who was dying admitted that she had a dream recently and, in the dream, she saw Jesus and her grandfather – who was involved in Freemasonry. Jesus told her in the dream that the reason she had gotten sick and was not getting healed was because of her grandfather! After she became aware of what the Lord showed me, she planned to order my book *Restored to Freedom* so she could read about why men who joined the Freemasons often times have people in their lineage that suffer terribly with back and neck pain, cancer, and other debilitating diseases due to the secret oaths that they make to Allah and curses to Jesus. Invariably you will see many people who drive vehicles that have the Freemason license plate logos on them parked in handicap parking spots. Thus, the dream that the woman had of Jesus telling her that she could not get healed of cancer because of her grandfather was exactly right. She needed to break off the curse from the sins of her grandfather over herself and bloodline which are outlined in my book *Restored to Freedom* which explains in detail about Freemasons and what is done behind closed doors (in secret) and why so many families that have a father, grandfather, or great-grandfather in that organization suffer tremendously with diseases and back and neck pain and worse.

I have seen so many people in my Healing Rooms who have suffered from tremendous back and neck pain, scoliosis, cancer, etc., that immediately gain freedom after reading the generational curse, Leviathan, and Jezebel renunciation prayers. There is life and death power in your tongue and when you speak out – you take the authority that Christ gave you and you will see miracles in your life. As you can see, it is so important to live a pure and righteous life and if we can align our lives with the Lord, we can reverse the curses we have been living under by breaking them off by reading the following renunciation prayers. It is time to stand up and take back from the enemy what has been stolen from you. It is time to be God's man and no longer allow yourself to be controlled by the enemy. Stand up and be counted by your heavenly Father and watch your life change in powerful ways. On the following pages are the renunciation prayers to break off generational curses, the Leviathan, and Jezebel spirits.

Prayer to Break Off Generational Curses

I break all curses or vows that have ever been spoken over me from my mother and father, and from all generational curses that have been spoken over anyone in my ancestry - all the way back to Adam and Eve.

In Jesus Christ's name, I declare that I am not in agreement with any form of sin or disobedience that operates in this world and against the throne of God, as I am not in agreement to any person or family member who deliberately sinned or perverted God's ways. In the mighty name of Jesus Christ, I thank You Father God for Your good and righteous ways and I seek to live my life by Your Spirit and reap the rewards of living by Your righteousness.

I repent for every relative connected to my family ancestry who has deliberately, or without spiritual wisdom - sinned against my Lord or His people. I realize that all sin will be judged one day and that each one of us is accountable for what we have said or done, but I am repenting for my family's sins in that I shall be released from any curses these sins may have produced against me. I put all of my sins and my ancestors' sins at the foot of the cross and declare that Jesus Christ has paid the price and that Father God - You have forgiven us for all.

I break all generational curses of pride, lust, perversion, rebellion, witchcraft, idolatry, poverty, sickness, infirmity, disease, rejection, fear, confusion, addiction, death, and destruction in the name and by the blood of Jesus.

I curse all traumas in my ancestors' and descendants' lives that have had any right to me and command all memory of these to be forever forgotten and never remembered again. I replace these traumas with peace. I speak that any and all nightmares in sleep will be turned to joy, loving dreams, and visions from the Lord.

I renounce the behavior of any relative in our family background who has lived more for the world than for God. I renounce any ungodly beliefs, traditions, rituals, or customs that my people may have followed or acted upon. I repent of those family members who sought to fulfill the selfishness of their desires, and those who have perverted God's righteousness, for I myself choose to serve God and live by His ways.

I declare that my descendants will receive blessings and favor from this day forward and that we will be blessed with love, joy, and peace throughout our lives and that Jesus will be the King of our lives. I declare life and health to me and my family line, right down to our very DNA - in Jesus' mighty name!

Amen.

On the following page is the Leviathan spirit renunciation prayer (much more information is in my *Restored to Freedom* book about the spirit of Leviathan, as well as the Jezebel spirit):

Prayer to Renounce the Leviathan Spirit

Lord, I come before you with a humble and contrite spirit, and command all spirits of pride to be gone from me forever in Jesus' name. I ask you God to remove from my life any influence from the spirit of Leviathan. I reject this spirit completely with all my heart and command it to be broken off me forever and to never return. Forgive me for any ways that I have served this spirit either intentionally or inadvertently. Forgive me for any ways in which I have been twisted or have twisted the truth, and for any ways that I have listened to distortion of the truth or have distorted the truth. I devote myself to bringing unity, not division or confusion - into the church and into my personal relationships and will therefore honor other godly members and those you have placed in authority over me.

It states in Isaiah 27:1, "In that day the Lord with His severe sword, great and strong, will punish Leviathan the fleeing serpent, Leviathan that twisted serpent; And He will slay the reptile that is in the sea." I declare that Leviathan is severed from my life now and forever more. By your grace, I will speak the truth in love and dedicate myself to expressing the truth of your word in my life and have a humble and contrite spirit in the precious name of Jesus. Amen."

The final renunciation prayer that is a must to breaking free from the Ahab spirit is on the following page and needs to be read in all seriousness in order to command it to be gone. Remember that life and death is in the power of your tongue.

Prayer to Renounce the Spirit of Ahab

Father in Heaven, I come to You in the name of Jesus Christ, my Savior and Lord. Father, it is my desire to see Your Kingdom come into my life and into my marriage (or future marriage) and into my family in a new and powerful way. Right now, I make a decision to forgive anyone and everyone who has had any influence in my life to cause me to be less than the person of God You wanted me to be. Father, I forgive the following persons who have unfairly controlled me (name anyone who comes to mind).

I repent of being like an Ahab and ask You to forgive me. I now take back the authority and responsibility You have given to me that I relinquished to Jezebel. By the power that works in me according to Your strength and anointing, I will watch over and minister to my new husband or wife in Christ, and my children. Father, I ask for wisdom and guidance as I do this. I speak a spirit of boldness and confidence in my life to be restored.

In the name of Jesus, I break every curse that has come upon me or been spoken over me and my family because of the influence of the spirit of Jezebel within my wife (or husband) and any sins of ours or our ancestors. I command every evil spirit that has come in through curses that I or others have spoken over me to leave me. Go out of me, now - in the name of Jesus Christ! You must also loose my wife (or husband), and family. I say to you, evil spirits - GO! I declare that I am bold in the Lord and command restoration of everything that the spirit of Jezebel has done to hurt me. I am blessed and highly favored and am strong in the Lord, and decree that my future life will be far greater than my former. As a believer in Jesus Christ, I have been granted the same authority as Christ and declare divine health throughout every cell in my body. I have the mind of Christ! I will help others that I know to become free from every spirit of Jezebel and spirit of Ahab, and decree that I will have a strong anointing over those spirits the rest of my life.

Thank You Father, for deliverance and healing, both now and in the days to come. I praise Your Holy Name! AMEN.

So the impact of generational curses and blessings was so important to be aware of, and being affected by our relative's sins that the Bible revisits this again in Deuteronomy below:

Deuteronomy 5:9-10 NKJV,

"⁹ you shall not bow down to them nor serve them. For I, the Lord your God, am a jealous God, visiting the iniquity of the fathers upon the children to the third and fourth generations of those who hate Me, ¹⁰ but showing mercy to thousands, to those who love Me and keep My commandments."

The Lord talks about the generational curses twice in the Old Testament and as you can see, we need to break off the right that those curses have to attach themselves to us. There is tremendous freedom when we finally break free from all spirits that are not of the Lord in our lives. We can finally start to transform into who we really are in Christ.

CHAPTER 8

Changing Your Mind

Mindsets that have been in place for a lifetime can, many times - take longer to change once you have been set free from the demonic spirits that have been afflicting you forever. I have seen people who are instantly changed and then on fire for the Lord. This chapter will focus on how to successfully change your old carnal mindsets of weakness in your flesh, to becoming a bold lion of Judah for God as your spiritual mindset blooms into its proper place.

The first thing to understand is what exactly is a mindset? A mindset is an existing way of thinking that you have had in place for a long, long time. Janie Baer does a great job of explaining the difference between having a carnal and a spiritual mindset.

I want to establish in this writing there are only two mindsets we can have. We can either have a carnal mindset or a spiritual mindset. What is the difference between a carnal and a spiritual mindset and what are the results we can expect from each? Here's a scripture giving us a clear description of both and the results for each:

Rom 8:6-8 KJV, "[6] For to be carnally minded is death; but to be spiritually minded is life and peace.[7] Because the carnal mind is enmity against God: for it is not subject to the law of God, neither indeed can be.[8] So then they that are in the flesh cannot please God."

This scripture tells us to be carnally minded is enmity against God. Carnally minded people have a real dislike or distaste for God, for His spiritual laws and principles (which is displeasing to God), and can result in spiritual death which is living a life separate from God, or even an early physical death. This scripture also reveals to us that being 'spiritually minded' pleases God and will lead to life and peace. Isn't that what every person desires, a good life and peace?

What does it mean to be carnally minded? It means to cater to the appetites and impulses of one's human nature, which is displeasing to God. Carnally minded is thinking and doing what is right in one's own eyes, which is humanism. To be carnally minded means to be facts minded, senses ruled, emotions driven, and controlled by sin, demons, and natural circumstances. Carnally minded means your thought process is generally what you can naturally expect. If you want to get down to the truth of it, to be carnally minded means you have a mindset that is contrary to God, His Word, His will for your life, and His planned outcome for you in any situation. With the carnal mindset, the Word of God is not reasonable. The carnal mind always is focused on the facts and focused on the problems only getting bigger with little to no way out! The carnal mindset is always what you naturally can expect which isn't much or is too little too late. Carnal minded thinkers are always victims and never victors.

On the other hand, I define being spiritually minded as being Spirit of God led and guided instead of reasoning led and guided, Word of God minded, craving for God and God's purposes, and satisfied with nothing less than God's perfect will for your life. A spiritual mindset is nourished by intimate times with God and meditation on the Word of God.

Ps 42:1-2 KJV, "As the heart panteth after the water brooks, so panteth my soul after thee, O God. 2 My soul thirsteth for God, for the living God."

Jer 15:16 KJV, "Thy words were found, and I did eat them; and thy word was unto me the joy and rejoicing of mine heart. . ."

Spiritually minded means you have given the Holy Spirit control of your thinking. Spiritually minded, you keep yourself focused on the Word of God for the answers which produces real lasting peace and clear answers and right direction.

Col 3:15 AMP, "And let the peace (soul harmony which comes) from Christ rule (act as umpire continually) in your hearts [deciding and settling with finality all questions that arise in your minds, in that peaceful state] to which as [members of Christ's] one body you were also called [to live]"

Spiritually minded means with the Word of God, you have developed such an image of victory that every problem, every frightening detail, and every fact and circumstance stacked against you loses any hold of your thinking. Spiritually minded is a person flowing easily in love, joy, peace, patience, kindness, goodness, gentleness, faithfulness, and self-control of the spirit because the Holy Spirit is the strength that produces these spiritual fruits.

A spiritually minded person allows Christ to conquer every temptation, test, or trial - because of their reliance on the Spirit of God to overcome all evil with good.

A spiritual mindset is the mind of Christ in operation and is not dependent on mere human wisdom, insights, and reasoning which have all kinds of limits and no real answers. Even in the church, we have relied on our intellect, human reasoning, and have been senses driven rather than living out of our spirit. This has closed off the Holy Spirit speaking to us through our spirit and what to do with all the facts and circumstances weighed against us each day. We have missed out on revelation, knowledge, and discernment by our spirit through our spiritual senses.

We are either being carnally minded or spiritually minded because there is no "in between." You either have the mindset of the natural, carnal world and you are facts concentrated and reasoning prone resulting in natural expectations or you give place to the mindset of the spirit which is based on the truth of God's Word and your expectations are supernatural coming from a higher dimension or the heavenly realm. This is why 2 Cor 10:5 should be a part of our thinking process every day,

2 Cor 10:5 KJV, "Casting down imaginations, and every high thing that exalteth itself against the knowledge of God, and bringing into captivity every thought to the obedience of Christ."

We must take every thought captive, check every thought to see if it is fact based, circumstantial evidence based, or if it is of the truth of God's Word. The Word tells us in 3

John 2 that we will prosper in all areas of our life as we prosper in our soul, and the soul can only prosper when it is centered on the truth of God's Word and the voice of the Spirit of God rather than on circumstantial evidence or the facts.

Carnally minded or spiritually minded - which will you choose in any given situation? You have to make the choice every single day. Being spiritually minded, our outcome will not be based on carnal thinking, facts, figures, human reasoning, and so forth but instead on the truth of God's Word. That's why we have to check out every thought to see if it lines up with the Word of God (which is the truth about us) and see if it lines up with what Christ's finished work accomplished for us.

The First Man, Adam brought us so low to living life according to human reasoning, the facts, the circumstantial evidence, the natural, and the carnal thinking possibilities that what we could naturally expect. Jesus brought us back up to spiritual thinking, spiritual possibilities, supernatural possibilities, heavenly possibilities, and heavenly intervention.

The carnal mind is sense ruled and is enmity against God and His Word and always will be.

Rom 8:7-8 KJV, "[7] Because the carnal mind is enmity against God: for it is not subject to the law of God, neither indeed can be. [8] So then they that are in the flesh cannot please God."

What does enmity mean? It means extreme hatred. The carnal mindset is enmity against the Word of God. Could this be the reason we have felt, at times - like the Lord is a million miles away when we have needed Him the most? We have chosen natural solutions to our situations because that made perfectly good sense. This is how most of us have been trained from childhood. What makes natural, good common sense does not make spiritual sense and is what I am trying to tell you. Enmity means we have chosen to be carnally minded about things even after we have prayed and confessed the Word of God over and over and over, and again and again. My friend, this is a futile practice. Carnal thinking and natural ways of handling things after prayer and confession of God's Word will prove to completely nullify all our prayers and all our confessions of faith. Natural sense does not ever make spiritual sense.

Solomon said it so clearly, so precisely,

Eccl 1:14 NLT, "I observed everything going on under the sun, and really, it is all meaningless--like chasing the wind."

Eccl 1:14 DRB, "I have seen all things that are done under the sun, and behold all is vanity, and vexation of spirit."

Solomon, a very wise man, tells us here in this scripture that he has observed the busyness of humans on the earth, their human thinking, reasoning, striving, and human desires - that are all just mere vanity and all of which vexes their spirit. They are doing all without the consultation of their spirit-man that is led by the Spirit of God. Their spirit is vexed day after day after day; thus – anxiety, weariness, and meaningless living sets in that leads many times to an early death.

The Church has to realize that a carnal mind vexes our spirit as Eccl 1:14 clearly tells us and our spirit was designed to know God and be led by Him. Unfortunately, many people (including Christians) are leaning towards the human mind, human reasoning, human training, humanistic ideas, and human ways of dealing with things (what naturally you can expect), and thus missing out on the spirit life of the supernatural and righteousness, peace, and joy in the Holy Spirit.

Human reasoning is resulting in many governments defaulting financially. These governments can't pay their bills, and even financial institutions are collapsing. Why? Because in their reasoning, they forgot God. Additionally, they have left God and God's financial principles out of the government. They tell you that there must be a "separation of church and state" and so they have separated themselves from God and spiritual answers that are the real answers they need to fix the problems with that they face. They have forsaken spiritual wisdom and spiritual direction in their finances and instead, have clung to and leaned on only the reasoning of their mind; and Solomon calls this "chasing the wind." This leads not only to the downfall of a nation, but also the destruction of lives of individuals, whole families, and even in the Church!

Romans 8:8 tells us they that are in the flesh cannot please God. This means that person is so carnally minded (naturally minded), that their faith is inoperative and destroyed, and this is displeasing to God. Now God has no choice but to allow that person to get what they expected in their carnal mind and reasoning, even though they prayed and confessed the Word of God. Most of the time, God will get the blame for their devastating outcome.

Again, if our soul is prospering with carnal reasoning, then that is what we will get; but if our soul is prospering in the truth of God's Word, then that is our outcome. We can pray and confess the Word all we want, but have a continual carnal mindset followed by corresponding natural speaking and natural actions - this nullifies faith and all our prayers and confessions. We can only change our results by changing our carnal mindset to a spiritual mindset.

The carnal mindset reasons away what is rightfully ours in Christ Jesus, for it just doesn't sound reasonable. This reasoning keeps us running to the world for our health care. Human (natural reasoning) is why the Church, along with the rest of the world - is so dependent on the Babylonian financial world system to borrow money. This is why we run to the world and in doing so, we don't see demonstrations of Kingdom health care and provision. You just can't mix the two kingdoms and expect to get Kingdom of God results. The Church must have clarity on this!

The carnal mind, or to be carnally minded, means you are only willing to see things in terms of the flesh or how things seem in this natural world. Therefore, a carnally minded person will probably tell you they will not believe it unless they can see it, or there is physical evidence of it. You hear people say, "The facts are the facts" like there is no other truth but the facts.

The truth is, the Word of God is the truth no matter what the facts tell us in any given situation. I know some would say, "Jane, you just can't deny the facts." I would tell them, "So are you telling me that I have to deny the truth of God's Word about this situation?" Actually, we must drop the facts if we are to believe the truth of God's Word and get its results. It doesn't seem reasonable, but the only way to get results the Word of God produces is to use the Word of God as the basis for everything in our life.

An excellent example of what I am talking about is when a doctor gives you his or her diagnosis; do you receive that diagnosis as the truth about you? You have to make a choice between the diagnosis or the truth of God's Word. I know he or she is your doctor, but they are only humans telling you what they humanly have discerned, which is their diagnosis; but then you will have to make the choice between human discernment or the truth of God's Word.

What about when you heard you were healed by the stripes of Jesus, did you instantly take that as the truth about you? We are talking about truth versus facts. We all have to choose daily between the facts and the truth of the Word of God because our outcome can come only from one or the other.

For the most part people (including Christians), because of their carnal programming - believe the diagnosis or facts the professionals showed them before they believe the truth of God's Word about them because again, they can see it, feel it, and heard it from a doctor who's considered the professional. Some people (including Christians), are so convinced everything their doctor says is law and gospel that they believe they can't do anything until they first have consulted their doctor. Consulted with whom? What about consulting with the Spirit of God or the Word of God and believing fully and faithfully what you heard from His Spirit or His Word? I don't think this even enters into the minds of Christians because they have been so programmed that they must consult their doctor and other professionals in this Babylonian world system before they can do anything and to them, the professionals' word is their final authority. It's like they are the ultimate authority on everything, yet they are just practicing medicine, practicing law, etc. The lawyers are practicing law, yet Christians will seek a consultation with a lawyer before they even think of getting counsel from the Holy Spirit or the Word of God (or a man/woman of God) about a matter. These professionals are practicing on your health and practicing the outcome of your legal matters which could affect your prosperity, your family, and your future. In other words, that's both dangerous and deadly. Need I remind you that "practice" means repeat something to get better or improve performance and is why they say, "Practice makes perfect." Practicing with your health and legal matters makes the practice of these professionals of medicine and law better.

Because of natural training and natural programming, the thought never enters the minds of Christians that the ultimate authority they should be seeking is the counsel of the Great Physician who knows all about their body because He is the Creator of it. The Holy Spirit (aka: the Great Counselor of all counselors) is available for consultation 24/7, and His legal consultation costs you nothing. Both physical and legal outcomes in these consultations would be accurate and would be far more advantageous every single time.

Carnal thinking destroys faith in the reality of God's healing and God's counsel and destroys faith in His promise of giving them an expected end. We must change from a carnal mindset to a spiritual mindset where we are pleasing the Lord because we are no longer cutting Him off from working in our affairs. Through natural carnal thinking, we keep the resurrection power of the Holy Spirit from giving life to every cell of our bodies where the curse of sickness and disease can't stay any longer. Through the counsel of the Holy Spirit, we gain the right legal action to take because He doesn't have a law degree in just one area of law.

Because Christians are so naturally programmed with this carnal mindset, they are prone to think and speak accordingly. How many times in a day or week do you come in contact with a Christian and the first thing that comes out of their mouth is usually something negative about their health. This is carnal thinking and carnal speaking. I mean, you could remind them they were healed by the stripes of Jesus, but then in the next second of time - they are back to telling you just how bad their health is and it's only going to get worse or their doctor told them, "You will just have to live with this for the rest of your life." Because of their carnal (natural thinking), they think nothing about how their speech is going against the truth of God's Word and actually nullifies its powerful ability to bring real change. They would fight you over the facts and

102

what they are doing, knowingly or unknowing – is choosing the facts instead of the truth of God's Word.

It is sad to me that I can engage in conversation with a Christian and most of the conversation is along the lines of carnal (natural thinking), and when you try to change the conversation to spiritual truths that would help this individual, they quickly change the conversation. These same Christians who were so heavily engaged in that natural (carnal conversation) will tell me they have to go, and they must leave now! They seem so uncomfortable with the truth of God's Word. Now that is sad to me.

I'm telling you, every Christian should have their thinking so changed to a spiritual, supernatural, and heavenly mindset that as we engage in conversation - we have very little (if any) natural conversation. We should be reminding each other of the divine health we possess, the divine prosperity that's part of our spiritual inheritance, and the quickening of our bodies by the Holy Spirit who raised Christ from the dead. When we become older adults, we should be sharing testimonies of how the Word changed situations and share the deliverance the truth brought into our lives. These are the things every Christian's conversation should concentrate on, and then I believe a spirit of faith would arise and there would be more demonstration of the power of God in the Church and not just in a church building, but everywhere the Church goes.

Isaiah 50:4 NKJV, "The Lord God has given me the tongue of the learned, that I should know how to speak a word in season to him who is weary. He awakens me morning by morning, He awakens my ear to hear as the learned."

Carnal words cause us to become wearier, hopeless, helpless, and anxious. Spiritual words build us up, edify us, cause faith to arise, cause hope to leap with fervent expectancy, spring forth joy, saturate with peace, and anchor the soul - resulting in encounters of God's presence, His power, and His glory.

Oh, that the body of Christ would set their minds on things above that are eternal and not on things of the earth that are temporal, when all are subject to change. If only we would set our conversations on spiritual things that change fear to faith, hopelessness to a hope with expectancy, conversations that destroy anxiety, and change worry to answers to all problems. Wow! That's the capability of spiritual conversations - to bring forth answers to unsolved problems and alleviate all anxiety, doubts, and fears! Conversation of the truth of God's Word is what is needed in the Church instead of the facts and circumstantial evidence which only generates more worry, fear, doubt, stress, etc. This is what would separate true believers in Christ from the world because we would be walking in the light of the Word of God and the discernment of the Spirit of God which would result in a demonstration of the supernatural this world is looking for. Spiritual conversations among believers day to day with faith declarations included would change a life, change a whole nation, change a whole generation set for failure, change our faith level, and even change our whole perspective of life to the "good life" promised in the scriptures. Oh, that we Christians would make the choice every day to choose a spiritual mindset and engage in conversations focused solely on spiritual truths.

In the Old Testament the Israelites were to focus their thoughts and conversation on the Law of Moses day in and day out:

Deut 6:7 NKJV, "You shall teach them diligently to your children, and shall talk of them when you sit in your house, when you walk by the way, when you lie down, and when you rise up."

Oh, that Christians today would choose to focus their thoughts on the truth of God's Word and talk it in their house and daily use the Word in their conversations with others and meditate on the Word as they go to bed and when they arise, fill their day with the truth of God's Word. I believe we would change the world in no time and be known as they were in the Book of Acts, "those who turned the world upside down!" Don't we want to be world changers today? It starts with choosing a spiritual mindset programmed by the Word of Truth, the leading of the Spirit of God, resulting in spiritual conversations, actions of faith, and divine intervention and demonstration.

Every Christian has to make a choice between a carnal mindset or a spiritual mindset every single day. Now that you know the difference, which will you choose: a carnal or a spiritual mindset?

As you choose to become more spiritually aligned with the Holy Spirit, you will have desires that are of the spirit and not of the flesh as sin will no longer be attractive. As your old carnal mindsets begin to break off you and your spiritual eyesight is able to see and sense things in the spirit - you will be transformed into the powerful and mighty man of valor that you are called to be. It is amazing to be able to start sensing things in the spirit as you will know how to talk to someone, know what they are able to receive vs. what they cannot. You will have spiritual wisdom from the Holy Spirit and be so much more effective when talking with people about the Lord, as well as hearing clearly from the Lord to be able to give words of knowledge and prophetic words to bring people into their destinies. Your spirit will come alive as you are able to think clearly in the Lord and no longer like the old you that was clueless in spiritual things.

As you shift your mindsets from the wrong thinking of your past to the correct thinking in the spirit, you will feel such freedom for the first time in your life. Every day, you will get up and feel drawn to the Lord and Holy Spirit. You will want to press in and receive a word from the Lord over yourself to see what the Lord wants to tell you to direct you. I receive words from the Lord that I write down in my journal on a regular basis, and it is so amazing to look back at various times in my seasons of life to see what the Lord told me. Most words were very comforting and many were words that gave me direction as to what to expect. Several were words that brought me immediate peace instead of feeling uncomfortable in worry or fear. I would encourage everyone to regularly keep track of a journal in your lives and then look back periodically to see what was going on during the various seasons of your spiritual journey. I have personally kept a journal every day of my life since April of 2007 in a Microsoft Word document (I write them down for a calendar year and then start a new document, so I can go back to a certain year and search for items more easily). It is very interesting to turn back and read about one of the days in my life that was extremely challenging and remember how hard a certain situation was during that day. It helps me to know that I should always be at peace and never be in worry or fear ever, as those are the enemy's ways. It is helpful to look back and realize that worry or fear never produced a second of peace, so you might as well stop worrying because that will not ever do you any good either. You are on enemy territory when you are in fear and you cannot maintain faith that the Lord will provide or protect you when you are constantly in fear. The Lord said He will fight your battles and be your provision so why worry for even one second about your life or your children's lives? Declare powerful words of prayer over your situation and then count it all done that the Lord will do the work and take care of things. Rest and sleep easy at night knowing that God has got it all. It is time to shake off the enemy from your life and change all your old mindsets from the past to the new wineskins of your future. Peace is a very good thing to constantly be in.

CHAPTER 9

Transformers

So how do you transform your desires from those of the flesh to things of the spirit? How do you get yourself jump started out of the old life and mindsets into being on fire for the Lord and having a real, tangible relationship where you hear from Him and get directed every day? You need to ask the Holy Spirit to help you. When Jesus was leaving this earth He told us that He would send a Helper to us. This Helper will change your life in such amazing ways that you will wonder why you never received it much earlier in your life. The Holy Spirit will guide you through every decision that you need to make which is critical so that you can rest assured every day that you are making the best decision for you and your family.

John 14:12-31 NKJV

The Answered Prayer

"¹² Most assuredly, I say to you, he who believes in Me, the works that I do he will do also; and greater works than these he will do, because I go to My Father. ¹³ And whatever you ask in My name, that I will do, that the Father may be glorified in the Son. ¹⁴ If you ask anything in My name, I will do it."

Jesus Promises Another Helper

¹⁵ "If you love Me, keep My commandments. ¹⁶ And I will pray to the Father, and He will give you another Helper, that He may abide with you forever— ¹⁷ the Spirit of truth, whom the world cannot receive, because it neither sees Him nor knows Him; but you know Him, for He dwells with you and will be in you. ¹⁸ I will not leave you orphans; I will come to you."

Indwelling of the Father and the Son

¹⁹ "A little while longer and the world will see Me no more, but you will see Me. Because I live, you will live also. ²⁰ At that day you will know that I am in My Father, and you in Me, and I in you. ²¹ He who has My commandments and keeps them, it is he who loves Me. And he who loves Me will be loved by My Father, and I will love him and manifest Myself to him."

²² Judas (not Iscariot) said to Him, "Lord, how is it that You will manifest Yourself to us, and not to the world?"

²³ Jesus answered and said to him, "If anyone loves Me, he will keep My word; and My Father will love him, and We will come to him and make Our home with him. ²⁴ He who does not love Me does not keep

My words; and the word which you hear is not Mine but the Father's who sent Me."

The Gift of His Peace

[25] "These things I have spoken to you while being present with you. [26] But the Helper, the Holy Spirit, whom the Father will send in My name, He will teach you all things, and bring to your remembrance all things that I said to you. [27] Peace I leave with you, My peace I give to you; not as the world gives do I give to you. Let not your heart be troubled, neither let it be afraid. [28] You have heard Me say to you, 'I am going away and coming back to you.' If you loved Me, you would rejoice because I said, 'I am going to the Father,' for My Father is greater than I."

[29] "And now I have told you before it comes, that when it does come to pass, you may believe. [30] I will no longer talk much with you, for the ruler of this world is coming, and he has nothing in Me. [31] But that the world may know that I love the Father, and as the Father gave Me commandment, so I do. Arise, let us go from here."

The most impactful way that you can become transformed in your walk with the Lord into who you really are in Christ is to utilize the gift of the Holy Spirit and praying in tongues. Being a Christian without the gift of tongues is like fighting in a war without a gun or ammunition to kill your enemy. You are at such a disadvantage against the enemy because you are not operating in your full battle ready state, and cannot discern things in the spirit realm. You are like a walking zombie that is dead on the inside. When you receive your prayer language, you get on fire for the Lord as your spirit aligns with Christ's and the enemy realizes that you are no longer the same person who was defeated and under his feet. You are the head and not the tail and when you pray in your prayer language, the enemy cannot speak to you at all because it circumvents your thinking mind and activates your spirit man.

One of the most notable men who has ever lived is quoted in the Word of God as saying, "I thank my God I speak with tongues more than you all," (1 Corinthians 14:18 NKJV). This was the incredible Apostle Paul who declared how important speaking in tongues was and if a man who wrote more of the New Testament than any other thought it was important enough to pray in tongues more than anyone else, what do you think that says to the rest of the world? The tenacious Peter also spoke in tongues and ministered this experience to others everywhere he went as it was key to getting as many believers to become activated in the Spirit so that they could do the same miracles, signs, and wonders like all the other disciples did. Those gifts did not just die out with the few disciples or those at Pentecost - they continued in the lives of all Christians that wanted all the gifts available to them to this day. Even the most important man of all – Jesus Christ, prophesied, "they shall speak with new tongues," (Mark 16:17) so if Jesus said it, then you better believe it because that settles it for me. Of course, the enemy would not want you speaking in tongues because if you do - you will be able to reign over him in power and authority and defeat his tactics at every turn. The enemy would want you to believe that it was only for the disciples, or that it was actually from the enemy which is so ridiculous.

Simply speaking, Peter and Paul benefited enormously by speaking in tongues. These two dynamic men of God, as recorded in the Scriptures - paint a moving example for the reader of how impactful the role of speaking in tongues played in their life. If they spent so much time talking about the benefits of it in the Word, then you can expect that we all better be doing it in order to be fully and completely activated to do what Jesus did. Do you want to be halfway armed to fight the enemy or do you want to be fully armed? Do you want to allow the enemy to beat you at every turn and live a defeated life, or do you want to put him on the run everywhere you go? It is time to put on the full armor which includes praying in tongues every day for the rest of your life to cause the enemy to run from you.

There are numerous benefits for the believer who speaks in tongues. This chapter presents a wide-ranging list, including comments on how much speaking in tongues can affect the walk of a believer in a most powerful and life-changing way. The goal of this chapter is to help you understand the benefits as to why it is so important because the enemy does not want anyone to pray in tongues so that they can only operate in a very limited fashion and not bring as many people into the understanding that they can do all things in Christ and walk in the miracles, and signs and wonders that all believers can operate in when they are praying in tongues. The enemy wants believers to just go to church, not learn about having an authority to command sickness to go, or to walk in any power and ultimately only bring a few to heaven with them while being a spiritual weakling all the days they exist on earth.

We will first discover how Peter and Paul benefited greatly from speaking in tongues and then we will witness the many ways listed in God's Word of how speaking in tongues can help you. It is very important to get this valuable information into your spirit so make sure when you are reading this that you are in a quiet place of solitude and without distractions because the enemy will not want you to understand this in your spirit and will cause interruptions to occur to stop you receiving what the Lord wants you to have. You may need to turn off your phone so you will not receive texts, calls, or Facebook messages because believe - the enemy does not want you to receive this and will do everything to distract you and stop you from getting this information into your spirit.

The Apostle Peter

Peter was one of the twelve disciples when on that most significant Day of Pentecost, he and others, "... were all filled with the Holy Ghost, and began to speak with other tongues, as the Spirit

111

gave them utterance" (Acts 2:4). At that time, there was chaos with many thousands of people trying to understand what was really going on. Can you just imagine what it must have been like for all those around them hearing them speak in other languages that they had never spoken before and how several who were from other countries could understand what they were saying at that time? It had never happened before in the history of the world, so how could people explain what was happening?

It took Peter, filled with the gift of the Holy Spirit and having just spoken in tongues, to boldly stand before all the Judean leaders and everyone else who was visiting Jerusalem during this important feast celebration, to proclaim the truth. He had to try to explain to those who had not received tongues what was happening - which is like explaining quantum physics to a ten-year-old.

What is most fascinating is that just several days earlier, Peter (along with the other disciples) was behind closed doors, "where the disciples were assembled for fear of the Jews." (John 20:19). They thought they would be the very next ones to be crucified so were filled with fear and trepidation. Just a few days later, Peter was speaking in tongues, having been filled with the gift of the Holy Spirit and began dynamically accusing the Judeans of their murderous crime. The Holy Spirit and speaking in tongues literally changes the old timid you to become a bold lion with such confidence that nothing will stop you from doing what the Lord wants you to do no matter if you were scared to death before. It is simply fascinating to see people transform from a mild mannered, soft spoken and shy individual to an on-fire, fearless mighty man of valor - proclaiming the gospel and changing people's lives into what they are to be in Christ. The more that you pray in tongues, the bolder and more confident you will ultimately become in your life and be more effective against the enemy's tactics.

Acts 2:14 and 23: NKJV

"But Peter, standing up with the eleven, raised his voice, and said to them, 'Men of Judaea, and all who dwell at Jerusalem, let this be known to you, and heed my words. . .'"
" ...you have taken, and by lawless hands, have crucified and put to death."

Peter, fully inspired by the gift of the Holy Spirit, was preaching without notes and preparation. Many people were hearing the message of salvation for the very first time and Jesus Christ, crucified and raised from the dead, was being boldly taught. The results are: "the same day there were added unto them about three thousand souls" (Acts 2:41). What has been so interesting to me is that the Lord told me years ago that when I would start speaking to groups, churches, retreats, live television audiences, and conferences – I would never have to write down any notes in preparation of my speaking engagements as the Holy Spirit would tell me exactly what to say and how to say it. I have seen exactly that as everywhere I go, I am at complete and perfect peace and never prepare anything ahead of time and speak the Holy Spirit's agenda - not my own preconceived ideas. So many times, I would have messed up what the Lord wanted to do if I would have prepared an outline or message on my own in advance. Often times, people have preconceived ideas of what they think they should talk about while the Holy Spirit knows exactly what to say and do. For instance, I invited a prophet to come speak at my local church and at the end of her message - she called people forward who wanted to receive prophecies. She ended up having more than she could handle so she asked me if we should split up the people. She had a large contingency of people from where she lived that came and since I did not know them, I felt the Holy Spirit tell me that I should take them because the words that I spoke to them from the Lord would allow them to know that it was the Lord because I had no idea who they were or anything about their circumstances. One after the other, they kept coming to me and the Lord gave me insight over each one's situations and unique keys to their destinies, situations, or future direction. After it was all over, I had prophesied over about fifteen people and many came up to me and confirmed that the words I had spoken were truly from the Lord because only the Lord would have known the intimate details that I spoke out. It confirmed for them what was about to happen to them in their future with the Lord and it also confirmed to me that I was hearing the Lord's voice accurately. Had I ignored the Holy Spirit's leading, I would have missed it and could have told the prophet that she needed to prophesy over everyone or I could have had her prophesy over the people that she knew from her town and it would not have been as impactful because she already knew much about their lives.

What made the difference in Peter's life to change him from being full of fear and behind closed doors to boldly accusing the Judeans of murder? The only thing it could have been was Peter was filled with the gift of the Holy Spirit and speaking in tongues. Jesus Himself had told Peter and the other apostles that they would speak in tongues (Mark 16:17) but you can imagine that they had no idea what He was talking about. Just before ascending on high, Jesus' last words were: "But you shall receive power when the Holy Spirit has come upon you; and you shall be witnesses to Me in Jerusalem, and in all Judea and Samaria, and to the end of the earth" (Acts 1:8 NKJV). The power they demonstrated was that they spoke in tongues and this occurred on the Day of Pentecost. Therefore, speaking in tongues is extremely important for all believers to do. In my Healing Rooms that started in October of 2015, we regularly had believers receive this gift at all ages. We have seen 7 year olds and 70 year olds (and everyone in between) receive the gift, and it is a most beautiful thing to witness because all it takes is for the believer to start speaking out whatever comes to them and some develop their languages quickly - others receive their prayer language over time. One woman from California who wanted to receive her prayer language started out by only being able to say "M&M" and for weeks it was "M&M&M&M" so much that she was referred to by her loving godly friends as the 'M&M girl.' After a few weeks, she received her complete language while driving in her car and she had to pull over as she became so overwhelmed and could feel the presence of the Lord on her and inside all of her car.

Speaking in tongues was not a "one time" event that stopped as millions have received tongues to this day. Peter was called by God to minister to the Gentiles: Cornelius and his family. This record is in Acts (Chapter 10), and through a series of events - he traveled to minister to Cornelius and his household.

Acts 10:44-46

"⁴⁴ While Peter was still speaking these words, the Holy Spirit fell upon all those who heard the word. ⁴⁵ And those of the circumcision who believed were astonished, as many as came with Peter, because the gift of the Holy Spirit had been poured out on the Gentiles also. ⁴⁶ For they heard them speak with tongues and magnify God."

One of the most dynamic leaders to live in the Christian Church was Peter. God had Peter write the Word of God in what we have today as I and II Peter. It should be very clear that one of the most important things he ever did was speak in tongues. If speaking in tongues was beneficial for Peter, it most definitely will be good for us. I believe that it is an absolute must in order to operate in what the Lord truly intended all believers to do because otherwise, they are not all there. Without it, you are just a very robotic and plain vanilla believer who does not have the fire within to do all that the Lord has called you to do and you are an ineffective Christian who does not have the full power from the Lord.

The Apostle Paul

The Apostle Paul went from murdering Christians to actually becoming a Christian. As a Pharisee, he exercised great power and heavily persecuted the Christian Church. In the book of Acts (Chapter nine), Jesus Christ came before him in a vision and changed his life. He became the great Apostle Paul, who grew to become the most influential leader in the First Century Church. God had him write much of the New Testament, including Romans, Corinthians, Galatians, Ephesians, Philippians, Colossians, Thessalonians, Timothy, Titus, Philemon, and Hebrews.

Within the Word of God that Paul wrote, God directed him to declare, "I thank my God, I speak with tongues more than you all" (I Corinthians 14:18). Speaking in tongues was obviously extremely important to Paul as he wanted to make sure that everyone knew he spoke in tongues more than anyone else that he knew. It allowed him to become the man of God that he was with all boldness and no fear. Again through the inspiration of God, Paul declared, "I wish you all spoke with tongues..." (I Corinthians 14:5). He would later write in the Word of God, "...do not forbid speaking in tongues" (I Corinthians 14:39). Paul was adamant that all Christians should speak in tongues so if you do not - I would plead with you to ask the Lord for the gift so that you can become a powerhouse for Him.

Not only is Paul recorded making these favorable statements about speaking in tongues, but he also was involved with helping people to receive their prayer language. In the book of Acts (chapter nineteen), Paul came to Ephesus finding some whom had not manifested the gift of the Holy Spirit. They were born again and filled with the Holy Spirit but had not received it into manifestation by speaking in tongues. During the early Church, it was normal for people to speak in tongues right after confessing Jesus as Lord and confirming their belief that God raised Him from the dead (examples of this are on the Day of Pentecost where they spoke in tongues and in chapter ten when Cornelius' family spoke in tongues right away).

We have also seen many children at our church that asked Jesus to come live in their hearts and then wanted to receive their prayer language and received it as we prayed for them.

When Paul arrived in Ephesus, it became evident they had not spoken in tongues. In this case, he ministered to them to help them speak in tongues because it was so critical that they operate in the highest level to be the most effective Christians that they could be. How many people do you know who call themselves Christians that do not speak in tongues? What are they like? They are usually subdued and unable to discern things of the spirit and thus - not as powerful when it comes to the spirit as those who do pray in tongues. Also, those who have the gift of tongues but do not pray in them every day are unfortunately unable to be on-fire for the Lord. I see these people every day and when you are around a person who prays in tongues regularly - you can feel the excitement level in their spirit and it becomes contagious because you just want to be around them because it rubs off on you.

Acts 19:6 NKJV

"And when Paul had laid hands on them, the Holy Spirit came upon them, and they spoke with tongues and prophesied."

If the great Paul spoke in tongues more than anyone else; and if he encouraged others to speak in tongues often; and if he told the Christian Church not to forbid speaking in tongues - it becomes quite evident to the Christian believer how vital speaking in tongues really is. It is just ridiculous that anyone in the church would argue against someone regularly praying in tongues since Paul was adamant that everyone pray in them. The enemy is definitely against people receiving their prayer languages.

Peter and Paul were the pillars of the early Church and an important part of their life was speaking in tongues. It was a big deal for them and if we are to model our lives after great men like Peter and Paul - speaking in tongues will be a most desirous action. The one man every Christian person would want to emulate is Jesus Christ and who told his followers that they would be doing great signs and miracles, including speaking in tongues (Mark 16:17). You, too, can speak in tongues like Peter and Paul did; and not only are you able to, but you really should in order to be the most effective Christian you can be. It is far too critical not to and their example alone is proof enough of how speaking in tongues is so dynamic and beneficial.

Benefits of Speaking in Tongues

You will discover that speaking in tongues is one of the most exhilarating, and soul satisfying actions you will ever do. As you learn the many benefits of speaking in tongues, you will also rejoice in the privilege God has set before the Church that they could have such a beautiful means of communicating with Him and praying for others. It's the full knowledge that you are a child of God, a joint heir of Jesus Christ, having access to all that the Lord has access to.

No greater feeling have I ever experienced than realizing I was born again, a child of God, and a joint heir with Jesus Christ. I received my prayer language at the age of 13 when my grandmother prayed over me in the farm house where I grew up. It raised my awareness in the Lord to a whole new level, and made it more genuine to me than just going through the motions of attending a church. There was no denying that there was so much more to this Christian life because I was now able to speak in tongues just like those in the book of Acts. I felt like I had tapped into a whole new level of power that I had never been exposed to before in my life, yet I was not quite sure what to do with it.

Speaking in tongues was proof enough for Peter (and his Judean followers) that Cornelius and his family - despite being Gentiles, were born again. When they heard them speak in tongues, they could not deny the tangible proof that when people were filled with the Holy Spirit - they would speak in their own unique prayer languages. This was the example that other non-Jewish people needed to know about to have no doubt that the Lord wanted all believers to have the gift of tongues.

Romans 8:16-17 NKJV

"[16] The Spirit Himself bears witness with our spirit that we are children of God, [17] and if children, then heirs—heirs of God and joint heirs with Christ, if indeed we suffer with Him, that we may also be glorified together."

The only act of the Spirit bearing witness with our spirit is speaking in tongues. What a wonderful reality our Heavenly Father has put into place by which we can have the proof in the senses realm of the spiritual reality of being a son of God and a joint heir with Christ. When you pray in tongues, you become one with Christ in a way that is impossible to do on your own. Your mind cannot get in the way when you are praying in tongues to stop what the Lord wants to have done. It is just your spirit and Christ getting into sync and in such a powerful way that's truly amazing.

To edify or build you up

One of the great benefits of speaking in tongues is that it edifies and exhorts you. There have been many times when I was discouraged about my circumstances, and when I began to pray in tongues - my entire countenance would change to positive again. The world is always trying to tear us down and the enemy is trying to whisper and speak to us to get us worried and in fear. There were many that I had counseled across the country who had not spoken in tongues before and were being pummeled by the enemy in their everyday thoughts. I would help them receive their prayer language and then teach them that every time they would get in fear or hear the enemy speaking to them - start praying in tongues. Every time they would do that, they would immediately stop hearing the enemy's voice to cause them fear and returned them back to a place of peace again. God's manifestation of speaking in tongues is always there to build us up and bring us into peace.

1 Corinthians 14:4 NKJV

"He who speaks in a tongue edifies himself, but he who prophesies edifies the church."

Jude 1:20 NKJV

"But you, beloved, building yourselves up on your most holy faith, praying in the Holy Spirit (which means speaking in tongues)"

To speak to God directly and speak divine secrets

People today want to talk directly to God and they want to hear from Him and this is exactly what speaking in tongues does. It is the spirit in you speaking to God. You will also be able to hear the Lord speak to you in your own language (on a consistent basis) which brings you even more peace knowing you can ask Him for insight any time you need it.

1 Corinthians 14:2 NKJV

"For he who speaks in a tongue does not speak to men but to God, for no one understands him; however, in the spirit he speaks mysteries." How incredible is our Heavenly Father to allow us to speak mysteries or divine secrets with Him. That is exactly what the above verse is declaring. We have direct access to God Almighty. It is our spirit talking to God who is Spirit (John 4:24).

To speak the wonderful works of God

God's Word declares that when we speak in tongues, we are speaking the language of men or angels (1 Corinthians 13:1). The speaker does not know what he or she is saying but as one speaks, God has designed it that one is speaking the wonderful works of God. We are not speaking wasteful words of gossip or speaking out our fears giving them life, but instead - we are speaking the wonderful works of God. How loving it is of our Heavenly Father to allow us to speak this way.

Acts 2:11 NKJV

"Cretans and Arabs—we hear them speaking in our own tongues the wonderful works of God."

To magnify God

When a person wants to express himself to someone he really loves, he may come to find it difficult to come up with the appropriate words. We love our Heavenly Father so much and desire to say just the right words to praise Him and when we speak in tongues - we are speaking words that magnify Him. What a privilege we have to express ourselves in the best manner possible by speaking in tongues. I enjoy my worship times with the Lord every morning and when I go on walks - I always pray in tongues. I work out at LA Fitness several times a week and since late in 2015, learned that I could go into a squash / racquetball court or a larger aerobic room (when not being used) and turn on praise music and walk around the room praising the Lord and speaking in tongues. Sometimes I would even see feathers as evidence that the angels were there with me enjoying the time of worship and prayers going up. It is so calming and energizing at the same time. I would highly encourage everyone to pray in tongues every morning and throughout your day for at least an hour, and watch what happens to your life. You will watch yourself transform into who the Lord has called you to become.

Acts 10:46 NKJV

"For they heard them speak with tongues and magnify God."

To pray perfectly

There are many times we do not know what to say in prayer. Our infirmity is that we just can't come up with the correct words to say. When we speak in tongues, our prayer is perfect because it is that perfect Spirit from God praying and we are so fortunate to have this power of prayer when we pray for others and come before the Father. It is the Spirit that makes intercession for us according to the perfect will of God and gives us the words to speak through the spirit abiding in us. Our limited minds cannot get in the way to try to figure things out in the flesh and we need to get our minds out of the way in order to allow our spirit to function perfectly and do the will of the Father.

Romans 8:26-27 NKJV

"26 Likewise the Spirit also helps in our weaknesses. For we do not know what we should pray for as we ought, but the Spirit Himself makes intercession for us with groanings which cannot be uttered. 27 Now He who searches the hearts knows what the mind of the Spirit is, because He makes intercession for the saints according to the will of God."

To worship God truly with the spirit

There are a number of ways in the Old Testament that God was worshipped. These include: singing, praising, giving thanks, and magnifying Him just to name a few. In the New Testament, Jesus Christ introduced another preferred way of worshipping God. When you are praying in tongues every morning - you feel the joy of the Lord and want to praise the Father for every good thing that He is doing in helping you become more like Him. It makes your worship time extra anointed in a way that otherwise is not possible.

John 4:23-24 NKJV

"²³ But the hour is coming, and now is, when the true worshipers will worship the Father in spirit and truth; for the Father is seeking such to worship Him. ²⁴ God is Spirit, and those who worship Him must worship in spirit and truth."

According to E.W. Bullinger in *Figures of Speech Used in the Bible*, the words "in spirit and in truth" (verses 23 and 24), are a figure of speech called hendiadys and is where two words are used, but only one thing is meant. Bullinger translates verse 24: "They that worship God, who is spirit, must worship Him with the spirit, yes – really and truly with the spirit."

How can a person worship God with the spirit? The only way logically is speaking in tongues. We have already seen the phrase "praying in the spirit" - which indicates speaking in tongues. When you speak in tongues, you are speaking not unto men but to God (1 Corinthians 14:2). Other Scriptures within this chapter indicate that speaking in tongues magnifies God and gives thanks well to God. It makes sense that to worship God with the spirit would have to be speaking in tongues. Philippians refers to 'worship in the spirit' and it is the perfect prayer.

Philippians 3:3 NKJV

"For we are the circumcision, which worship God in the spirit, and rejoice in Christ Jesus, and have no confidence in the flesh."

People talk about doing worship services, which usually means singing or praising. This is nice, but what our Heavenly Father prefers is worshipping Him truly in the spirit, which is speaking in tongues. Have you ever attended a church that does not operate in the gift of tongues and then attended a church that fully operates in tongues? You can just feel the difference. One church feels like they are dead while the other is on fire for the Lord.

To give thanks well

The more I learn of God's awesome love for us, my heart pours out with appreciation. What more thanks can I express than to use what He has given to me? What touches the heart of a parent is to observe their children utilizing the gifts that we give them. This is so true with the Heavenly Father and someone once said, "God's heart melts when He hears us speaking in tongues."

I Corinthians 14:15-17 NKJV

"[15] What is the conclusion then? I will pray with the spirit, and I will also pray with the understanding. I will sing with the spirit, and I will also sing with the understanding. [16] Otherwise, if you bless with the spirit, how will he who occupies the place of the uninformed say 'Amen' at your giving of thanks, since he does not understand what you say? [17] For you indeed give thanks well, but the other is not edified."

The least we can do is speak in tongues much, which gives Him thanks as well.

To have the Spirit bearing witness with our spirit

The one action God designated that demonstrates that the Spirit is in us is speaking in tongues. God did not leave the spirit-filled believer without any tangible witness of His presence in us. The Spirit bearing witness with our spirit is speaking in tongues.

Romans 8:16 NKJV

"The Spirit Himself bears witness with our spirit that we are children of God"

We have the assurance of knowing that the Spirit of God resides in us. Hearing yourself speak in tongues verifies (in your heart) the spiritual realities of what God's Word declares. You have the proof that is undeniable and it matches up to the Word of God.
To make intercession in your prayer life for situations and for other believers is what we are called to do. This aspect of speaking in tongues is astounding and we can get a picture of someone in our mind and then speak in tongues for them. It is a perfect prayer in the spirit for others and there may be a situation where you do not know what is going on - but there is a concern and need for prayer. Instead of worrying about trying to find out what is going on, we can just pray in the spirit or speak in tongues and it is covered. How peaceful is it to know that you can intercede for someone perfectly without even knowing the details? God is so gracious by allowing us to just speak in tongues, and then He does the rest. In fact, they have done studies

on people praying in tongues today that they can trace back to an ancient Jewish language that was spoken when Jesus was alive. I tried this out one time when I met some Chinese students from Purdue at the Castleton Mall in Indianapolis. They needed some help with a car problem and as I assisted them, I learned they were Christians. I asked them if they spoke in tongues and they said that they did so I told them that I had acquired a second dialect (to pray in tongues), and I wanted to see if they could interpret what I was saying. I began to pray in tongues and they said that they could understand some of what I was saying. They said it wasn't Chinese, but some ancient Tibetan language. It was so cool to know that what I was saying could actually be interpreted.

Ephesians 6:18 KJV:

"Praying always with all prayer and supplication in the Spirit, being watchful to this end with all perseverance and supplication for all the saints."

The power of this kind of prayer is magnified in the above verse in Ephesians 6:18. Reading the context of this part of God's Word, we witness that we are in a spiritual battle. "For we wrestle not against flesh and blood, but against principalities, against powers, against the rulers of the darkness of this world, against spiritual wickedness ..." (Ephesians 6:12). The next several verses are the encouragement to "...take unto you the whole armor of God..." (Ephesians 6:13). What is so remarkable is that after putting on all the pieces of the armor, the one great act we do is pray in the spirit, which is to speak in tongues. This is how immensely powerful the manifestation of speaking in tongues is. So pray in tongues as much as you can, and watch how you transform into a mighty man of valor that can move mountains with your faith.

To be a sign to unbelievers

Unfortunately, today, when someone hears another person speaking in tongues - people question, "What is this weird activity?" This is the poor state into which our world has developed and for those who are hungry for the truth, it will perk up their curiosity to check it out. For those who will not believe, this will seem crazy. For those who will believe, it is a sign of the Spirit of God in manifestation.

I Corinthians 14:22

"Therefore tongues are for a sign, not to those who believe but to unbelievers; but prophesying is not for unbelievers but for those who believe."

Mark 16:17 NKJV

"And these signs will follow those who believe; In My name they will cast out demons; they will speak with new tongues."

How many demons have you cast out of someone? I had not cast out one from anyone until 2009. I have now cast out and led people through prayers to cast out over hundreds of them to allow people to be truly free from the torment of the enemy. So many Christians are under such bondage in their spirits from the enemy. It is such a privilege to do what the Lord has commanded and such a blessing to see so many get set free from lifetimes of slavery and pain. I have also rarely seen a demon manifest in my presence because they know that I know my authority as a believer and they must respect me. I have had several who have felt the effects of demons trying to choke and stop them from reading the renunciation prayers to get free from the Jezebel and Leviathan spirits in my book *Restored to Freedom*. It is so important to know your authority in Christ – my book *Jesus*

Loves To Heal Through You would be an excellent resource to learn about your authority.

Acts 2:11 NKJV

"Cretans and Arabs - we hear them speaking in our own tongues the wonderful works of God."

Jesus Christ declared that the sign to look for would be speaking in tongues (Mark 16:17). People ought to listen to our Lord and Savior and heed his words. When the visitors to Jerusalem witnessed these Galileans speaking their language, it perked up their soul and got them to listen. It is a rest and means of refreshment to the soul because it is a sign of having salvation in Christ.

Hundreds of years prior to the Day of Pentecost, it was prophesied that there would be a language spoken that would sound like stammering lips. The results of people speaking like this would actually bring rest and a refreshing to the soul.

Isaiah 28:11-12 NKJV
"[11] For with stammering lips and another tongue He will speak to this people, [12] to whom He said, 'This is the rest with which you may cause the weary to rest,' And, 'This is the refreshing'; yet they would not hear."

Paul refers to this Isaiah record while writing I Corinthians 14:21 and 22.

I Corinthians 14:21-22

"²¹ In the law it is written: 'With men of other tongues and other lips I will speak to this people; and yet, for all that, they will not hear Me,' says the Lord. ²² Therefore tongues are for a sign..."

The record in Isaiah was a prophecy foretelling that speaking in tongues would be the rest and the refreshing. Paul was demonstrating this truth in 1 Corinthians 14:21 and 22. What was occurring during Isaiah's time was that the leaders of Judah were ridiculing Isaiah for treating them like children. They were promoting their works above God's and as a result - the children of Israel could not enter into the rest God promised them because of their unbelief.

Today, speaking in tongues is the proof to believers that they have made Jesus Lord of their lives and have entered into God's rest. We have ceased from our works trying to reconcile ourselves back to God and have recognized the full and complete salvation work of Jesus Christ on our behalf. Because of God's grace and mercy, we have entered into the family of God. As we speak in tongues, we are reminded of this and therefore have the rest and refreshing of God.

To bring a message from God or for God (when interpreted) to the people who are gathered in a group

Speaking in tongues is a part of another manifestation that brings an edifying message to the listeners that will comfort or exhort them. The following verses demonstrate what exactly this wonderful manifestation does and how it is to operate in the Church.

1 Corinthians 14:5, 13, 27

"⁵ I wish you all spoke with tongues, but even more that you prophesied; for he who prophesies is greater than he who speaks with tongues, unless indeed he interprets, that the church may receive edification."

"13 Therefore let him who speaks in a tongue pray that he may interpret."

"27 If anyone speaks in a tongue, let there be two or at the most three, each in turn, and let one interpret."

The purpose of the manifestation of prophecy is similar to the purpose of the manifestation of tongues with interpretation. If someone speaks in tongues in a meeting, that person should interpret the message as God gives them the interpretation. The message is not for the individual but solely for the body of believers as they fellowship and meet together. This manifestation of prophecy builds up the listeners with its message as does the manifestation of interpretation of tongues. Whenever tongues are prayed out loud by one person in front of an audience, someone should always interpret in their language, so everyone can know what the Lord said.

To experience possible health benefits

There have been several research studies that suggest benefits to the immune system during speaking in tongues. Other studies have indicated very interesting brain activity during speaking in tongues.

The mental health that comes with the assurance of knowing you are born again of God's Spirit and that you have a proof that is undeniable can't help but give a person a wonderful feeling. To know you are rich with Christ within and you are heaven bound and all hell cannot stop you from going - definitely gives you confidence and peace.

Conclusion

It is amazing how much speaking in tongues benefits the believer. Peter and Paul spoke in tongues much and experienced its benefits in their ministries throughout their lives. Jesus Christ would not have foretold of speaking in tongues unless there was a significant purpose for it (Mark 16:17).

My prayer is that believers will experience the many astounding benefits of speaking in tongues as I have, as well as those who I have helped receive their prayer language. My prayer is that through speaking in tongues - they will experience the reality of knowing they are children of God and joint heirs with Jesus Christ; that they will be edified; that they realize they are speaking directly to God, and speaking divine secrets to Him; that they know they are speaking the wonderful works of God; that they know they are magnifying the Father; that they are praying perfectly; that they are giving thanks well; that they realize they have the witness of the Spirit within; that they can make intercession in their prayer life for situations and for other people; that they show themselves to be a sign to unbelievers; that they have the rest and refreshment to their souls; that they can also operate the manifestation of tongues with interpretation; and that they experience possible health benefits. May the truth of God's Word prevail in your life and may you speak in tongues as much as possible every day of your life!

I have seen that many people who hear from the enemy (who experience fear, doubt, and anxiety) that pray in tongues literally takes them from a place of fear - to peace and confidence. I recommend whenever you are sensing that you are getting into fear or worry, to immediately pray in tongues and away your worries will go. The enemy simply cannot speak to you to cause you fear when you are praying in tongues because it blocks the enemy's voice from coming through. I was working with a woman from Florida who heard from the enemy frequently. When she decided to receive her prayer language, she learned the benefits quickly because every time the enemy spoke to her causing her to start to fall into fear, she would pray in tongues and the enemy could no longer speak to her. This allowed her to receive tremendous peace.

I love this article below by the late Rev. Kenneth E. Hagin concerning his experience with speaking in tongues. In this article, Rev. Kenneth E. Hagin shares about the moment he was filled with the Holy Ghost with the evidence of speaking in other tongues. He also teaches about one of the major benefits of doing so. Below:

As I knelt on the living room floor of that Full Gospel parsonage, I just closed my eyes and shut out everything around me, and I lifted my hands to God. No one told me to do it; I just lifted my hands (that's pretty good for someone who was untaught).

I said, "Dear Lord, I've come here to receive the Holy Ghost." I repeated in my prayer what I had just learned from Acts 2:39 and Acts 2:4. Then I said, "Your Word says that the Holy Ghost is a gift. Therefore, I realize that the Holy Ghost is received by faith. I received the gift of salvation by faith. I received healing for my body three years ago by faith. Now I receive the gift of the Holy Ghost by faith. And I want to thank You now, Heavenly Father, because I receive the Holy Spirit."

Then I said to the Lord, "By faith, . . . I have now received the Holy Ghost. Thank God, He is in me, because Jesus promised it in His Word. And I say it with my mouth, because I believe in my heart that I have received the Holy Ghost. Now I expect to speak with tongues, because believers spoke with tongues on the Day of Pentecost. And, thank God, I will, too, as the Holy Ghost gives me utterance."

After I had prayed that and because I was grateful for the Holy Ghost whom I had just received and for the speaking with tongues that God was going to give me, I said, "Hallelujah,

hallelujah" but I had never felt so "dry" in all my life saying that word.

Feelings and faith are far removed from each other; in fact, sometimes when you feel as if you have the least faith - that is when you have the most faith because you do not base your faith on feelings. I said "Hallelujah" about seven or eight times, even though it seemed as if that word was going to choke me!

About the time I had said "Hallelujah" seven or eight times, way down inside of me (in my spirit), I heard some strange words. It seemed as if they were just going around and around in there and it seemed to me that I would recognize them if they were spoken, so I just started speaking them out!

So about eight minutes from the time I first knocked on that pastor's door, I was speaking in tongues! The pastor had said, "Wait" but instead of waiting - I spent that hour and a half before the church service speaking in tongues! It is much better to wait with the Holy Ghost than to wait without the Holy Ghost!

I believe in waiting on God, of course. We should have tarrying meetings for people who are Spirit-filled. It is more wonderful to tarry and wait in God's Presence after you've been filled with the Holy Spirit than it is to wait in God's Presence before being filled with the Spirit.

Also, notice that you don't speak in tongues and then know you have the Holy Ghost. No, you believe you have the Holy Ghost first, and then you speak in tongues. Notice Acts 2:4: "And they were all filled with the Holy Ghost..." If we stop reading there, we know that they were all filled with the Holy

Spirit but if we continue reading, we find, "…and [they] began to speak with other tongues, as the Spirit gave them utterance" (Acts 2:4). Speaking with other tongues was a result of those believers having received the Holy Ghost. You receive the Holy Ghost first; then you speak in tongues.

During that hour and a half that I was speaking in tongues, I had a glorious time in the Lord. You see, speaking in tongues edifies you as 1st Corinthians 14:4 says, "He that speaketh in an unknown tongue edifieth himself…" Therefore, speaking in tongues is a means of spiritual edification or building up.

Linguists tell us that there's a word in our modern vernacular that is closer to the meaning of the Greek word translated "edify" and that is the word "charge." We charge a battery; we build it up. Jude 20 says, "But ye, beloved, building up yourselves on your most holy faith, praying in the Holy Ghost."

In other words, when a person prays in the Holy Spirit, he charges himself up. He builds himself up like a battery that is charged or built up.

Edifying yourself by speaking in other tongues is just one of the many blessings that God has provided through the baptism in the Holy Ghost. This wonderful blessing, this glorious gift of the Holy Ghost - is available to every born-again believer.

Therefore, there is so much need for every believer to receive the gift of tongues and supercharge themselves to be on fire for the Lord. Why would anyone not want to be a major threat to the enemy, especially in these final days until the Lord returns to earth? It is time for you to transform into the lion that has been asleep in your life all these years. Let the enemy hear you roar!

CHAPTER 10

Walking in Authority

My life was changed forever when I began to learn in 2009 that I could walk in the same power and authority as Jesus Christ and see the same miracles that He performed. I transformed from a man who inherited the Ahab spirit from my father (and his father and so forth up the Schuman line) into an on-fire, Holy Spirit led, hearing the voice of God, mighty man of valor who was ready to take on the enemy in every capacity and defeat him everywhere I walked. If God can change me from a mild-mannered, going-through-the-motions church attender (who was a financial services technology executive) into a mighty man of God who now flows in the prophetic, deliverance, and strong healing ministry - then He can change you as well. It is time for as many men (and women) to transform into walking in the fullness of Christ every day of their lives. Getting direction from the Lord every day and night, sensing which way the

Holy Spirit is moving, and being a part of it is what it is all about. No more playing church and being a part of the walking wounded, zombie-like shells of men which are so prevalent today. We are coming into the end times of this world, and the tribulation is nearing. The harvest is ripe, and we need to be clean, pure, bold, and confident before the Lord and walk in our full authority in Christ.

Let me describe for you just who you can really become when you transform into the mighty man of valor that you are in Christ. Below are key points of what your life will become on an everyday basis:

1) **Hearing the Lord speak to you as often as you want to communicate.** He wants a personal relationship with you, and will give you direction and words of wisdom as much as you desire it. I have regular "conversations" in my mind throughout my day and it is so special that I would never go back to the old dead way of living with no relationship with the Creator of the universe. There is something special about asking the Lord a question or asking for insight about a certain matter and then hearing from Him and knowing that the choice you are making is the right one. When you walk every day conversing with The Mighty One and knowing He wants to talk with you - there is nothing like it in the world. You cannot help but want to change to become more like Christ.

2) **Staying in peace at all times no matter what the circumstances look like in your life.** Typically the Lord takes His people through times of having to trust Him to meet your needs instead of you providing for yourself in order to make you stronger against the enemy's tactics. In other words, when I used to make a lot of money in my job, I did not need to trust in the Lord. In order to get me to become closer to Him and have total reliance and trust in Him (and be in peace at all times) - I went through a season for several years of total dependence on the Lord to meet my financial needs. My heart

was to come into my own ministry, so I needed to transition from trusting in the world's ways and receiving money from my job into the Kingdom's ways and trusting that the Lord would provide for me. If you want to become more like Christ, you must learn to start living the way He did with total trust. Often times, you will need to experience some circumstances that may not feel pleasant for a season, but eventually - it causes you to change to become who you really are in Christ and it makes you stronger as the anointing on your life grows with it.

3) **Seeing others through the eyes of Christ.** To have the compassion that Christ has for others who are hurting and in pain requires that we experience people in our lives who have been hurt by the enemy through those in their lives and then see them as Christ does and love them accordingly. When you begin to take on the characteristics of Christ, you will sacrifice your own desires and wants for the good of others, and you will know it is the right thing to do in your spirit. When you can truly see others as Christ sees them, you will have tremendous patience for others' faults instead of speaking harshly to them like most in this world would. In my book *Loving Like Christ* - I talk extensively about how to do this, and it is not easy because everything in your old self will not want to tolerate having to sacrifice greatly for another. I know personally what it's like to go through this transition - it is one thing to see hurting people like Christ did but an entirely different thing altogether when it costs you everything you own. This is, however - what Christians are ultimately called to do which is to lay their own lives down for others.

4) **Praying in the Spirit (tongues) every day.** There is so much power that occurs when you pray in tongues for an hour or more a day. The enemy cannot speak to you when you pray

in tongues to cause you fear or anxiety and you will experience a peace and a power to which nothing else compares. Start your morning off with praying in the Spirit and watch what starts to happen in your life as the worries of the day will not hit you as you feel the Lord's presence and peace all around you. Throughout your day, continue to pray in the Spirit and you will feel such an amazing presence around you as you transition to becoming more powerful in the Spirit in who you are in Christ. If you do not have your prayer language, ask the Lord for it right now and start speaking out whatever comes to you and He will give you the desires of your heart. If it sounds strange at first, just continue to press in and over time - it will develop into an amazing prayer language that will take you places you have never been before.

5) **Learning and receiving into your spirit that you have the same authority as Jesus Christ and the disciples to heal the sick, cast out demons, and raise the dead.** I would highly recommend reading my book *Jesus Loves To Heal Through You* as well as Kenneth Hagin and Andrew Wommack's books which both have the same name called *The Believer's Authority*. I read both of Hagin's and Wommack's books and my life began to immediately transform as I saw an instant healing of a severe toothache. Two days later, I was healed of an excruciating pain in my back (over two days) after I heard a disc pop in the middle of my back as I bent down awkwardly over a gate to lift up a puppy. I also had a golf ball sized growth that later appeared a few years later in the center of my back (on my spine) and it took over 7 weeks to get healed as it finally dissolved slowly away. The Lord told me that as long as I did not get into fear, He would heal me of everything, every time - and He has kept up with His end of the bargain since June of 2009. I have been healed of everything and have

not taken any over-the-counter medications nor prescription drugs since that time. I also stopped taking all vitamins and supplements and have eaten a much healthier diet, exercise every day, and feel like I am in my 20's with so much energy and vitality. I have saved so much money from learning about my authority in Christ that it has truly been amazing for me to witness. It is not easy as the enemy will try to cause you fear and worry, and if you get into fear - you will have to go to the doctor for your healing because once you are in fear, you're on enemy territory and he has a right to keep you in sickness and disease. Also, you need to make sure to break off any generational curses from you and command any enemy spirits that have a right to you to be gone and stay pure of sin before the Lord as you cannot be looking at pornography or having relations with a woman who is not your spouse and expect to not open a door to the enemy to have a legal right to attack you. After a person becomes a Christian, the first thing they should learn is that they have the same authority as Christ (and the disciples) to command healings and help people get delivered from afflicting spirits.

6) **Stay Christ-focused every day and your fleshly desire for sin will fall off in time.** It is so interesting when a person chooses to commit their lives to the Lord in a stronger spiritual way. The enemy wants to keep them down and have them feel condemned about the sins of their past. The Lord wants to have you focus on Him and become who He sees you as. If you are a man, the Lord wants you to realize that past sexual sins do not define who you really are in Him. You are a pure and righteous man of God who is bold and confident in Him. As you draw closer to the Lord, your fleshly desires for sin will become less and less and before you know it - you will be transformed into the mighty man of valor that the Lord sees you as. When you break free from someone operating in the

Jezebel spirit, you will begin to have more peace in your life and the perverted sexual temptations will fall off with it. Keep the Lord first on your mind throughout the day, and you will be amazed that the sins of your past will no longer have the stronghold over you anymore. You will feel cleaner and more loving like Christ than you could have ever imagined.

7) **Read your Bible because you want to read it and not because you know you should.** You will desire to read the Word because you want to actually grow and become more mature and not because you know it is the right thing to do. You will want to read it because it comes alive and is more exciting to you and the Holy Spirit will help you see things that you never knew before. Ask the Lord for your spiritual eyes to become alive and watch what will happen. You will be able to comprehend (and understand) Scriptures like never before and if you are struggling to stay awake when reading or struggling to understand it - you most likely are being influenced by the Leviathan spirit and need to read the renunciation prayer that I included in Chapter 7. Also, you can learn much more about it in my book *Restored to Freedom*. Many may have grown up reading the King James Version of the Bible which is much more challenging to understand because of all the "thees" and "thous" so I would recommend that you read a version that is easier to understand. My personal preference is the New King James Version, but I also enjoy the Amplified and even the Message for further explanation in a different way.

8) **Watch videos / television and teachings of anointed men and women of the Lord.** I enjoy watching the Sid Roth show as he interviews guests who have had amazing encounters with the Lord. It causes my spirit to rise up and get energized to do

the same things that his guests have experienced in order to be more like Christ. Some of those that I enjoy watching and learning from include: Todd White, Kenneth Hagin, Bill Johnson, Robby Dawkins, Bob Hazlett, Glenda Underwood Jackson, Andrew Wommack, Tim Brown, Robia LaMorte Scott and James Scott, Danny Silk, Morris Cerullo, Reinhard Bonnke, Heidi Baker, Lance Wallnau, Joan Hunter, Joyce Meyer, Christian and Robin Harfouche, etc. It is very helpful to find people who have gone before you and are walking in the authority of Christ to watch and listen to their messages. There is something about learning from someone who is currently living today and following the Lord closely in their life because they are in the here and now and can share testimonies from what the Lord did for them. The Lord draws ordinary people to Him to do extraordinary things. It is also important to follow people who have no hidden sin in their lives and are the same person behind closed doors as they are in front of a pulpit. Yes, they are just people and they are going to make mistakes and as long as they are up front and open before the Lord and if they do make a mistake - apologize for it, repent, and grow closer to the Lord, then it is a good thing.

9) **Spend time around other men (or people) who are close to the Lord.** You should have a spiritual mentor who can speak into your life to help you grow in the Lord. Ask the Lord to direct you because it is very important that you do not follow someone who does not operate in all the spiritual gifts or has hidden sin in their lives. If you are a man, then you should have a man as your mentor. If you are a woman, then you should seek out a solid woman (that does not have the Jezebel spirit and wants to control and receive power over other people). Seek and you will find someone who is healthy for you as the Lord will bring them to you. Once you are stronger

in the Lord, you will be able to go to Him more and trust that He will direct you. Until you are at that place, you need to find a strong Spirit filled believer who knows about walking in the authority of Jesus Christ and operates in the healing, deliverance, and prophetic giftings.

10) **Find a Holy Spirit led church whose leaders are strong in the Lord and teach about walking in the same authority as Christ, utilize the gifts (healing, deliverance, and prophecy) and teach the whole truth of the Bible and not just love and grace exclusively, but also that there are consequences to behavior that is contrary to the Word.** It is so important to attend a solid church whose senior pastor is pure and righteous before the Lord, knows his authority in Christ, and whose prayers have results concerning physical healing, deliverance from demonic spirits, and speaking prophetically over people to lead them into their destinies. You need to see results from them and not just empty words. Be very careful not to put yourself under a pastor who is subtly controlling, anxious, angry, seducing, or exhibits any fruits outside of the healthy spiritual fruits listed in the Bible. The Lord will direct you if you should change to a church that is more aligned with the Lord and His ways. You do not want to attend a dead church that is all fire and brimstone, no flow of the Holy Spirit, or one that has "ultra-grace and love" messages that say if you go to hell - you can still get out one last time. You need to attend a church that speaks the truth about consequences for sin and behavior that is contrary to the Lord's ways. It must be balanced and teach the deeper truths in order to get you to the place that you need to be operating in to be most effective.

When you are walking in the power and authority of the Lord every day in your life, you will never want to go back to the old you. There is something so exciting about hearing the Lord's voice whenever you need advice or direction on something as it brings tremendous peace and confidence into one's life. When you have been set free from all enemy spirits that tried keeping you down (so you could not reclaim your position in Christ), you will feel so much more joyful and excited to love on others in the world who are hurting and depressed in order to bring them up to your level. Living a life in the power and love of the Lord is something that cannot be matched by anything on this earth. You can literally start to bring heaven to earth as long as you remain humble and pure before the Lord. Purity is something that will become you as the desires of the flesh fall off and the excitement of the things of the Spirit leap out of you. It is time for you to come into the full authority of the Lord in your life and start doing extraordinary things on a daily basis. Walk closer with the Lord every day and watch miracles happen wherever you go. You carry His presence with you and those that you come into contact with can literally feel it. It is such a blessing to take off the old you and put on the new and month after month, year after year - you become more like Christ every day. You can and must do it as your spouse, family, community and country depend on you. God is counting on you and is looking forward to seeing you reach your destiny and completing His calling in your life!

REFERENCES

Herbert Lockyer – All the Women of the Bible
Janie Baer – Carnal versus Spiritual Mindset
Kenneth E. Hagin – The Holy Ghost

FINAL THOUGHTS

Waking the lion within you must occur in order to activate the calling that the Lord has in your life. You are not a coward anymore and must stand up for what is righteous and change your life in order to be the mighty man of valor that the Lord expects you to be. There are millions and millions of men who have abdicated their authority in Christ that the Lord called them to have. For the sake of all men, it is time to stand up and be counted and walk forth in the boldness the Lord has called you to become.

If you would like me to speak and minister at your church, seminar or conference - you may contact me on my website. If the revelations in this book have helped you and changed your life or saved your marriage, you may wish to make a tax deductible donation to Restored to Freedom at http://www.restoredtofreedom.com which will help continue to get the message out to people all over the world that there is hope and a way to gain total freedom in Jesus Christ. Amen.

Made in USA - Crawfordsville, IN
52998_9781537006215
01.10.2022 1451